# MENTALLY BANKRUPT

## Running on Fear, Refueling with Faith

CAITLIN DALY

Manufactured in the United States of America

Scripture quotations from
https://www.biblegateway.com/ New International Version
(NIV) unless otherwise cited herein.



Published by Amazon KDP

ISBN: 9798394346330

# DEDICATION

To Jesus, for saving me and giving me my life back.

"But as for me, how good is it to be near God! I have made the Sovereign LORD my shelter, and I will tell everyone about the wonderful things You do."
-Psalm 73:28 (NLT)

# CONTENTS

# ACKNOWLEDGMENTS

First, I want to thank Jesus, my Savior, my Living Hope, my Healer, my Peace when the storm rages around me, the One who sees me, and most importantly, the One who remembered me. Lord, I am so blessed and thankful for every tough time because that is where I fell in love with everything You are. It is where our friendship grew, and my ride-or-die faith was established and solidified on an unshakable foundation. Through it all, I promised to never love You any less, and I am so thankful for this journey of life You have brought me through.

I want to thank my amazing daughter, Anthea, for showing compassion and understanding at such a young age as I went through the throes of anxiety and depression. I know this time wasn't easy for either of us, and I am so thankful for you. God knew what He was doing when He put us together, and I can't express how special you are to me.

I want to thank my mom, dad, siblings, extended family, and friends for praying with me, and for me, and for never leaving my side, always reminding me of who and Whose I was, especially when I was too tired to remind myself.

I want to thank Pat and Dan, two of the most outstanding Christian counselors, who have walked me through processing the murky waters of life. I don't know where I would be without you both, and I am so grateful that God allowed our paths to cross. I look forward to continuing our discussions in the years to come.

Lastly, I would like to thank my dear friend Marvina, who came into my life when all hope seemed lost. You have been God's vessel to give me hope and encouragement. I don't think I will ever refer to you other than "Marvina, my prayer warrior." The day I messaged the church desperate for hope, God allowed you to answer, and I will spend the rest of my life forever grateful for that day.

*"I sought the Lord and He answered me and delivered me from all my fears."*
–Psalm 34:4

# PREFACE: PURE PANIC

This book has been my survival story. It was written during a time in my life when everything was out of control. I had always considered myself an anxious person; however, at the ripe age of thirty-three, my anxiety and panic attacks took on a whole new level. Looking back now, I realize that sometimes God's only way of getting our attention is to take everything out of our control, so we can rely solely on Him. During this particular year, my family suffered loss, illness, housing issues, financial stress, health problems, and relationship turmoil.

As the pressure was building over the months, it finally came to a head for me when I had a low blood sugar scare that led me to believe not only was everything around me out of control, but now medically, I felt out of control inside my body. When you feel like you are out of control outside and inside your body, there is literally no escape. You live in a constant state of hell, waiting for the impending doom of something terrible to happen at any moment, and you physically can't escape it. I spent the next several months trying to constantly and obsessively manage my blood sugar levels. I went through bottle after bottle of test strips, monitoring my sugar levels day and night and pricking my fingers to the point that they were numb, bruised, and calloused. In light of my diagnosis of obsessive-compulsive disorder, my counselor concluded that I was hyper-focused on my blood sugar because it was the only thing I felt like I could control.

I was completely out of control. I gained over thirty pounds in just a few months and set alarms to wake myself up to eat throughout the night to stay "in control." If I woke up during the night, the first thing I would do was check my sugar levels. Even if they were in a normal range, I would still eat something, fearing the monitor was wrong. I was afraid to work out, I was afraid to drive without knowing what my levels were, I was afraid to leave the house, and most of all, I was afraid to live. Words can't describe exactly how mentally broken I was during this time. Whenever my body felt the least bit different, I panicked, fearing that this was the end...definitely the end.

If you have never experienced a panic attack, this may not make as much sense to you; however, if you have, I want you to know, I understand. You are not alone, and I can promise you I have been there in the depths, and I have also been on the other side, looking down on the fears that once consumed me. During this period, it was hard to find relatable stories of other people who suffered from panic attacks. Honestly, the only story that gave me hope was from the Christian singer Josh Wilson. I came across a three-minute and forty-two-second interview where he explained his panic attacks and his struggle with anxiety. He wrote a song called "Carry Me," which I listened to every time I felt overwhelmed, knowing he wrote the lyrics at a time of complete desperation—the same feeling I was experiencing.

Besides Josh, I had difficulty finding anyone who was just "real" about their experience, so I want to share with you what I specifically went through. I feel that if we aren't real in our words to each other, we will only isolate ourselves from each other more. As Christians, I don't believe that is what God would want us to do. So here it goes:

I would wake up in the middle of the night, multiple nights in a row, and immediately have an irrational negative thought come into my head. Then my heart would start racing (like 180 bpm racing). I would get so out of breath I couldn't breathe, which would panic me even more. I would literally throw myself into a cold shower (pajamas and all) to shock myself out of the panic attack, pacing around in wet pajamas, praying to God to just make it stop.

I have had to carry a brown paper bag because I would work myself up to the point of hyperventilating. I have used so much peppermint oil to help me calm down I'm surprised I can still even smell it. I carried a 'pulse ox' to check my oxygen levels (you know, just in case my asthma decided to turn against me). I couldn't sit through a meal without getting up at least two or three times to check a mirror and see if I was breaking out into hives or if my throat was closing up from a food allergy (one I knew about or a new allergy I wasn't aware of).

Heaven forbid I got a cold and needed to take medicine! I would agonize for hours and work myself up into a panic, fearing the medication might give me an allergic reaction. Sometimes it would take me a few days to even begin taking what the doctor prescribed (if I mustered up the strength to even take it at all). My daughter went to school late eighteen days in a row. I didn't get her fifth grade back-to-school picture until Day 5 of school because I couldn't physically get myself out of the car to take it. I would drive to work, sit in the car and sob uncontrollably. It took everything in me to walk into my office building.

I would go through periods of shaking and tremoring from the undercurrent of anxiety that built up in my body. I would lie in bed, heart pounding, tears streaming, praying for a miracle. I went through a period of four months where I would wake up at least three times a night in a completely panicked state, drenched in sweat, my heart racing, desperately pleading with God.

Most days I would be so anxious that I would cry uncontrollably, thinking, *God, how am I going to do this every day for the rest of my life?* I couldn't focus on those around me as hard as I tried. I was too consumed with a dread of impending doom that dominated every thought that entered my mind.

Going to the grocery store was nearly impossible. I anxiously fidgeted in my seat every time we went to the movies, unable to concentrate. Going out to dinner felt like a prison sentence. I would often be anxious about one thought, and then another would come into my head. If I was lucky, that new concern would replace the old one. Otherwise, the concerns would pile up until I felt like I was balancing a million different fears that raced through my head, all the while trying to complete the everyday tasks of being a wife, mother, and full-time employee.

The walk of anxiety and panic attacks can be very lonely. The isolation you feel when you are trapped in your mind, unable to escape your body, is arguably the worst experience in the world. I believe that the moments you feel most alone are precisely where satan wants you to be. "Alone" makes God feel a million miles away. When certain relatives and loved ones don't understand or don't seem to care, it isolates you even more, and depression starts to set in. The cycle continues until you feel so lost and broken that the way out is barely visible, a light in a never-ending tunnel that only shows a flicker of hope every few minutes.

At these moments and in these times, I would do my best to speak life and truth back into the draining reality I was experiencing. (ESV, Nehemiah 8:10) says, *"The joy of the Lord is your strength."*

Joy is strength, but how can you experience it when all other emotions press down on you like the heaviest weighted blanket you have ever felt? Words are easy to say, but living and believing those words is quite another task. I struggled with this for a *very* long time.

The Bible gives many examples of uncertain situations where there seems to be no way out, but God always made a way.

I discovered that the only way out is through and that's scary… that's actually extremely scary, and it's OK to admit that. There are so many times I started my journey through and went right back to my safety net of fear. So, if you have experienced that, please know you aren't alone, and it's alright because we're going to try one more time together and remind ourselves of all the brave men and women who went through some terrifying things in the Bible and came out on the other side, victorious in Christ.

My prayer for you, as you read the rest of this book, is that you find courage, that you find peace, and most of all, that you find the most incredible relationship with Jesus, a relationship that binds you for eternity and turns your struggle into an incredible testimony of survival. Over the next few chapters, the stories are intended to give hope, comfort, and freedom from panic, depression, anxiety and addiction, so you can live the life God intended you to live and send that panic right back to Hell, where it came from!

You got this!

We are in this together,

-Caitlin

# INTRODUCTION

We constantly hear the word "bankrupt," primarily associated with bank accounts, failed businesses, and loss of income. Webster's dictionary defines a person who is bankrupt in three different ways:

**1:** a debtor (such as an individual or an organization) whose property is subject to voluntary or involuntary administration under the bankruptcy laws for the benefit of the debtor's creditors

**2:** a person who becomes insolvent (unable to pay debts owed)

**3:** a person who is completely lacking in a particularly desirable quality or attribute

What if I told you that you could also be mentally bankrupt? I was going through a rough transitional time when everything was out of control. As I prayed and pleaded with God, the words "mentally bankrupt" came into my head. I started mulling over the meaning of the phrase and all the ways that it currently pertained to my life. In the first definition, we see that the focus is on an individual or organization whose property is subject to voluntary or involuntary administration.

What if I were to tell you that every time you put down your guard, every time you choose to put anything else above God, every time you allow negative words to come out of your mouth or negative thoughts to enter your mind, you are allowing the ultimate "creditor," satan, to go in and take un-rightful claim over your life? Galatians 5:1 (CEV) tells us, *"For freedom Christ has set us free; stand firm, therefore, and do not be subject again to a yoke of slavery."*

Christ set us free, but our job as believers is to "stand firm" and press forward beyond the old bondages that hold us back. We are given choices every day where we may ask ourselves, *Will I let this emotion dictate my response? Will I choose to be understanding rather than gossip about this person later? Will I choose to trust God at the onset of my negative thought instead of allowing it to enter and wreak havoc all day long?*

This first definition references voluntary and involuntary attacks on the individual who has gone bankrupt. In the financial world, we may or may not have a say in why or how we become bankrupt, but in the mind, we do have a say. It is important to note that when we stop catching our thoughts at the onset, we are involuntarily allowing satan to creep in and take claim. When we know the "right" response but choose to respond in the flesh versus responding with the wisdom of the Holy Spirit, we are voluntarily giving satan real estate in our mind, where he will take claim inch by inch. If that isn't anxiety-provoking, I don't know what is!

The downfall here is we are all human. I would love to say that I *ALWAYS* catch negative thoughts at their onset and respond with the wisdom of the Holy Spirit, but I don't, and that is OK, because you won't either. In fact, neither of us will get through an entire day without falling short, and that's where God is so wonderful. He already knew this! He loves us so much that before we were formed, He gave us His Grace, which basically means that He made up His mind before we sinned, that He would choose to bless us rather than give us the punishment that our sin deserves.

What a wonderful God we serve! Romans 3:23, in the Contemporary English Version (CEV), tells us, *"All of us have sinned and fallen short of God's glory."*

God doesn't leave it there though. He follows up with verse 24, *"But God treats us much better than we deserve, and because of Christ Jesus, He freely accepts us and sets us free from our sins."* Oh, how I love that verse! The difference one verse can make. In verse 23, we are told we will never measure up to what God calls us to be. Then we hear those fantastic words that resound throughout the Bible, *"But God..."* God never wants you to feel like His love is unattainable, that His ways can't be your ways, and that the path He set forth is so unbearable you ask yourself, *why bother trying?* No! He lets us know that although He is aware that we will never be perfect, He has already decided to treat us better, and not only better but with unconditional love. A love that caused Him to have His one and only Son die for us, that we can be forever freed from our sins and forever imperfectly perfect in His eyes.

So, although we inevitably will fall short and fail at keeping our guard up all the time against the adversary, take courage and remind yourself that an inch taken can also be gained back. It will take a lot of work and partnership with our Savior, but we can do this because Romans 8 reminds us, *"If God is for us, who can be against us?"* So, stand up. Take claim over God's anointed real estate in your mind, stop letting the involuntary and voluntary attacks take over your life, and let the battle begin!

Definition number two of bankruptcy is, "A person who becomes insolvent." Insolvent means that you are "unable to pay debts owed." Luckily for us, no matter how mentally bankrupt we are, if we are willing to accept Jesus as our Savior, rely on Him, and live the best life we can according to His word, we will never be unable to pay the debts owed from the shortcomings of our life. Jesus paid that price, and the only requirement for us is to accept, trust and love Him unconditionally.

I believe one of satan's strongest tactics in separating us from God is by telling us the lie that our sin is too great, we are too far removed, and too broken for God to care, love, or be concerned with us. The negative thoughts and lies about our life can enter quietly but build into giants that take over the space in our minds. We reach a point where we read the Bible or hear God's word but don't believe His promises are meant for us. We ask, how could they be? After all, we aren't one of His beloved characters in the Bible. We are broken and wavering in our faith at best when the storms rage around us.

This is where the mind needs to stay strong. Even if you are barely holding on and are trembling to get through the day, you remind yourself that no matter what situation or circumstance brought you to mental bankruptcy, you are choosing TODAY to take back the real estate of your mind. You are choosing TODAY to say, "Jesus, I trust You, and even though I have allowed the enemy to enter into my mind and I haven't always done everything the way I should, I know that today is a new day, and You already paid the price for my shortcomings; therefore, there is NOTHING that can separate me from Your unconditional and perfect love. What You have done for all the great men and women of the Bible, You will do for me because I am a child of God."

There is never a debt too great or small for Jesus to handle. The thoughts may pile up, and your stress may hit at a hundred million miles an hour. Take a breath and center your thoughts on Jesus and all the debts His blood shed on Calvary covered. You remind the adversary to Whom you belong, and every single debt has been recompensed. There is nothing that he can hold over you any longer. In the wonderful words of our Savior, "It is finished."

The third and final definition of bankruptcy can directly affect the mind in many ways as you deal with anxiety or any struggle in your life. This definition speaks of a person lacking a desirable quality or attribute. During the day-in and day-out battle with anxiety, there are many days when you will feel like you are not enough…not strong enough, determined enough, spiritual enough, patient enough; the list goes on and on.

We have already established that satan's primary target is our mind, so naturally he would take advantage of this angle of attack. When we feel we are lacking in any way, our normal human response is to feel defeated. When we feel defeated, we become depressed, and we speak negatively about ourselves to ourselves and to others. The thoughts spread to words, becoming the verbal version of how we view ourselves. This cycle continues and strengthens until we truly believe all the little lies that have settled in our mind.

This can be a tough challenge to confront because, by the time we get to where we realize there is a problem with all the negative thinking, we are so far down the rabbit hole we really need to focus in order to get out. The Bible gives us many verses to combat the feelings of defeat and lack in our lives. I highly suggest writing down verses that speak to you and your personal struggle and use them to talk back to the negative verbiage with which you have littered the prime real estate of your mind. Read them at the onset of every mental attack, and every time a negative doubting thought creeps into your mind.

A few verses to get started are the following: (NKJV, Philippians 4:13) assures us that He (God) is strong, so therefore in Him I am strong too. (Actual verse: *"I can do all things through Christ who strengthens me.")*

(NIV, Romans 8:37) declares He (God) is a conqueror, so therefore in Him, I am a conqueror too. (Actual verse: *"In all these things, we are more than conquerors through Him who loved us.")*

(NIV, Ephesians 3:12) declares, He (God) is capable and bold; therefore, in Him, I am capable and bold too. (Actual verse: *"In Him and through faith in Him, we may approach God with freedom and confidence."*)

(NIV, Romans 15:13) reminds us, He (God) has peace and joy, so in Him, I too have peace and joy. (Actual verse: *"May the God of hope fill you with all joy and peace as you trust in Him, so that you may overflow with hope by the power of the Holy Spirit.")*

Start building up your vocabulary with the word of God. Speak back assertively, aggressively, and with *all* the power bestowed on you from our loving Savior. (NLT, Romans 8:11) *"The Spirit of God, who raised Jesus from the dead, lives in you."* Brothers and sisters, let's start acting like we have some real power here! We aren't some poor, beaten-down, pathetic creatures. We are handmade in the image of God and have been given incredible power! A power that when we call on Jesus for help, the pure sound of His name causes EVERY knee to bow, in Heaven, on Earth, and under the Earth. (Philippians 2:10).

So, take a breath. Brush yourself off and start using that God-anointed power to reclaim what satan has stolen. God will give us more than we lost if we take a stand and put our faith in Him. (Deuteronomy 30:3-13).

In summary, when you are mentally bankrupt, you have depleted your savings (your spiritual and mental reserve, for lack of better words). Just like a bank account, if we don't continually deposit money, we will eventually hit a zero balance or, worse, a negative balance. Sometimes these withdrawals are minor; other times, we require a larger one. A spiritual and mental withdrawal could be any time you find yourself in a sticky situation and grasp what God would have you do or try to stand firm in what little faith you have built up.

It might be when you are given a choice to do what is morally right or wrong, and you try to pull the little information you have from your bible lessons as a child. It might be that a friend or loved one was in an accident, and you desperately start praying, even though you haven't spoken to God in years. Either way, if there aren't sufficient deposits, the account will suffer and deplete, making your withdrawals a struggle and giving you little to pull from and work with.

You are usually given a grace period when your bank account is over drafted. Then, if you haven't reconciled the amount overdrawn, you are hit with an insufficient funds fee. These fees will accumulate until your account is returned to good standing. If we expect to live victorious lives, our spiritual and mental account needs to be treated the same way. We cannot expect to occasionally go to church, check the box and go on our merry way as if all is fulfilled.

Could you imagine if you only went to work for one day and expected an entire paycheck on payday? You wouldn't know your job well, you wouldn't know the boss very well, and you certainly wouldn't have the skill set to successfully maintain your job against competitors. Keeping your spiritual and mental bank accounts full requires dedication, commitment, and perseverance. This means that we spend the day conversing with God, including Him in our day-to-day lives, just like we would a best friend. This means that we take time to read our Bible, join a study group or engage in spiritual discussions that will help us grow our faith and keep it strong. This also means we must take inventory of our lives and see exactly what can and should be weeded out.

Is there a friend group or relationship you know is a bad influence? Do you have lunch with the ever-entertaining but gossipy girls at work? Do you choose activities that, if Jesus were invited, you would turn fifty shades of red and pray to die on the spot? All these things can help increase or decrease your bank account's spiritual and mental balance. Take time every day to enhance your relationship with God. Your circumstances will drastically change, and you will start to feel spiritually and mentally wealthy and stable. You will suddenly have an entire workweek's balance deposited into your account. You would know the Bible and your identity in Christ well. You would get to know the boss (Jesus) really well.

Most importantly, you will have the skillset built up in your spiritual account to face anything the adversary throws your way. Really, you're doing yourself a favor! Anything God requires of us is always in our best interest; it's just our flesh that gets in the way. It's important to note that just as a bank account can incur overdraft fees, our spiritual and mental bank account can, too. Instead of an "overdraft fee," we can refer to it as "anxiety" or a "panic attack ." This can happen when we ignore the Holy Spirit's warning signs and continue to live the life we want instead of realigning our path to what Jesus wants.

About a year before I went through a very challenging season of severe panic attacks and anxiety, I kept hearing in my heart to *Read your Bible. Study your Bible. Open your Bible. Be in the word.* It was like little promptings, and I was so busy with life I just ignored the warnings. Long story short, exactly one year later, I found myself in desperate need of strength from the Bible, God, and His word. Had I followed the promptings of the Holy Spirit, I don't think my situation would have turned out as desperate as it did. It took me a long time to rebuild my mental and spiritual bank account to have ample reserve for satan's next attack.

Just as the bank sends notices as a "warning" that your account needs attention, panic and anxiety are also warnings that our spiritual and mental accounts need attention, and just like the bank, we are typically given a grace period to correct our actions and choose to take new steps to start to bring our balance back up to good standing.

Suppose you ignore these signals of anxiety and panic when your spiritual and mental accounts become over-drafted? In that case, the warnings will start to pile up, and eventually…well here you are, so I can almost guarantee you ignored the signals as I did. Don't worry, we're just going to go through the rest of your journey together and learn how you can replenish your spiritual and mental bank accounts, just like I did.

It is important to note that although we receive warning signals and alerts, God has given us free will, which means that before you go on, you will have a choice to make. Are you ready to go after God with everything you are in order to accept everything He has for you? This means facing your fears head-on. Being open and honest about your struggles. Being willing to go along the path the Lord has set before you to perfect you in a way you never could do on your own. Are you ready? Take a breath…let's begin.

# CHAPTER 1: WHO ARE YOU?

*"Life isn't always about finding yourself. It's about discovering who God created you to be."* - David A.R. White

Who are you? This is quite a loaded question. Every day, we can have many identities—mom, dad, sister, brother, son, daughter, husband, wife, boyfriend, girlfriend, caretaker, boss, employee, neighbor, friend, student, influencer, athlete, etc. There are so many ways we could identify ourselves that it's almost easier to list what we are not, and work backward from there.

Our identity is constantly questioned in the world in which we live. There are so many politically correct options now; even biological certainties are being challenged and made uncertain. In a world with so much confusion and chaos surrounding the simple question, "Who am I?" it is important to remember that knowing who we are is vital in standing our ground against the adversary.

Suppose we are uncertain of who we are at the core of our being. In that case, the enemy will have a field day as he prepares his attack, confusing us at every turn and making us question everything about ourselves.

The Bible has much to say regarding who and Whose you are. Before we get into the throes of dealing with our anxiety and panic, we need to establish a solid and unshakable foundation, so when we confront the enemy head-on and hit those weak days, we can brush ourselves off, step up for Round Two, and find confidence knowing who we are in Christ and exactly why the enemy will never win. So, without further ado, let's begin to unwrap what the wonderful word of God says you are, and there is no better place to start than at the beginning.

(ESV, Genesis 1:27), *"So God created man in His Own image, in the image of God He created him; male and female He created them."*

How incredible is that? God could have made us in the image of anything, and He chose Himself. God is perfect, which means that no matter what flaws you think you have, you are made uniquely perfect by the same hands that created the Universe. So let the flaws go and embrace you for who you are. There is a reason for every freckle, every blemish, and the chemical makeup God chose when creating you. Are you feeling special yet?

(NET, Jeremiah 1:5), *"Before I formed you in your mother's womb, I chose you. Before you were born, I set you apart. I appointed you to be a prophet to the nations."*

God knew you before you were ever placed in your mother's womb. Before you were even an idea or a thought on earth, you were a very special idea and thought in Heaven. This verse also tells you that you were set apart and appointed for a purpose. You are called to be strong and steadfast, and you can only do that if you recognize and acknowledge the incredible plan God has for your life.

Lastly, you were chosen. Say that again, "I am chosen." You are not an accident, you are not a mistake, and you didn't just happen by chance, no matter what your earthly story says. God had—and has—a unique plan for you, and He chose you.

(ESV, John 1:12), *"But to all who did receive Him, who believed in His name, He gave the right to become children of God."* This verse tells you that you are a child of God. I don't know your family dynamic; some of you may have been born into an unloving home, had to handle abusive parents, or got tossed around from foster home to foster home. The idea of a loving parent might be so far off that it isn't even a vocabulary word you would dare to use. This is where you find a key component of your identity. No matter what your experience with a parent or parents was, you now have an ultimate parent. Someone who calls you *His* child and *His* own. Embrace the fact that no matter how damaged relationships on earth have made you feel, you do have a Father in Heaven, and He is, in every sense, the perfect parent. So, child of the mightiest King, let's start acting like it!

(NLT, Galatians 4:7), *"Now you are no longer a slave, but God's own child. And since you are His child, God has made you His heir."* Not only are you a child of the Most High God, but you are also an heir to all the riches He has stored up in Heaven.

(NLT, Ephesians 1:3), *"All praise to God, the Father of the Lord Jesus Christ, who has blessed us with every spiritual blessing in the heavenly realms because we are united with Christ."* You are blessed. The blessings of God surround you. They are present when you wake up and present while you sleep.

(ESV, Deuteronomy 28:2), *"And all these blessings shall come upon you and overtake you if you obey the voice of the Lord your God."* That's a pretty hefty promise. First, you are blessed, and now you are blessed so completely, so fully, that as long as you obey the Lord, the blessings will overtake you. You can't outrun the blessings of God!

(CEV, Romans 5:17), *"God has treated us with undeserved grace, and He has accepted us because of Jesus. And so we will live and rule like kings."* You are accepted by the Creator of the Universe. Whenever you feel out of place, alone, or abandoned, you remind yourself that you are accepted. There is always a place for you with the Father, and no matter what you face here on earth, you belong to Him and with Him forever.

(NIV, Psalm 139:1-4), *"You have searched me, Lord, and you know me. You know when I sit and when I rise; You perceive my thoughts from afar. You discern my going out and my lying down. You are familiar with all my ways. Before a word is on my tongue You, Lord, know it completely."*

God knows everything about you. He knows your good days and not-so-good days. He knows when you're stressed and when you're excited. He knows the innermost thoughts that no one else knows and the struggles that no one else sees. On your best days, He rejoices with you; on your worst days, He consoles you. There is nothing that you can do that will take God by surprise. Take comfort in knowing that He loves you completely for exactly who you are; when you sin, He loves you; when you praise Him, He loves you. There will never be a time that our heavenly Father holds back His love for you. In essence, this is the ultimate relationship—to have someone know you so fully, so completely, and still love you despite anything you could possibly do. Rejoice! You are known!

(NIV, Romans 8:1), *"Therefore, there is now no condemnation for those who are in Christ Jesus."* This means you are forgiven if you seek forgiveness and live to love and serve the Lord. You are forgiven because the

Father, who knows all your secrets, also knows your heart and the deepest, most inner desires to be with Him. His forgiveness allows us to never be separated from Him or His love. Thank goodness for that!

(NIV, Romans 10:9-10), *"If you declare with your mouth, 'Jesus is Lord', and believe in your heart that God raised Him from the dead, you will be saved. For it is with your heart that you believe and are justified, and it is with your mouth that you profess your faith and are saved."* You are saved! Hallelujah... probably the best promise so far! Only two things are required here, and they are so simple. It's like God wanted to make sure this one was especially available to all: speak the truth that Jesus is Lord and believe in your heart that Jesus was raised from the dead. Thank goodness we serve a God Who doesn't give us impossible demands.

(NIV, John 8:36), *"So if the Son sets you free, then you will be free indeed."*

You are free! No matter what may be holding you back in your personal life, what your past says about you, or how chained you may feel to a certain situation or mental struggle, you are free. Jesus is here to save us from everything, including ourselves. Claim it over your life and declare it in the moments when you feel as if you are trapped in a circumstance. Christ says I am free, so I am free indeed!

(NIV, 2 Corinthians 9:8), *"And God is able to bless you abundantly, so that in all things, at all times, having all that you need, you will abound in every good work."* This means, brothers and sisters, that you are equipped to do all you need to do. God has blessed you abundantly, ensuring you have the necessary tools to go forward and abound in every good work. You might say, "Well, I have tried to do many things, and none of them have worked out, so how can this verse be true?" We must remember that the beginning says, "God is able." This doesn't mean He *will.* It also states that He will enable us to complete every "good work." You can't expect to live your life how you want and have God bless a plan that isn't His. Therefore, it is so important to pay attention and listen to the guidance of the Holy Spirit. God has a specific plan for your life, but to live it to the maximum capacity, you need to have a clear direction of where He is leading you. Then and only then will we be able to live the victorious life God has called us to live. How wonderful to know that no matter what life God has called us to live out, He enables us to handle it all with blessings and all the provisions we need.

(NIV, James 1:5) *"If any of you lacks wisdom, you should ask God, who gives generously to all, without finding fault, and it will be given to you."*

You are smart and not just smart but full of wisdom! There will be many times when you feel like you aren't the sharpest tool in the shed; we all have moments like that. Maybe you were the worst-performing student in school. Perhaps your friends always made fun of you because you lacked the intellectual depth that seemed to come so easy to them. We are all made up of different strengths, but one of the most wonderful gifts from our Heavenly Father is His ability to bless us with what we lack.

When you start studying your Bible, you will see that God never used the smartest, strongest, or bravest to accomplish His divine plan. He used the willing. James 1:5 assures us that it will be given if we ask, and the wisdom that comes from the Holy Spirit is available to all. So, the next time you feel like you are struggling to understand the depth of a particular situation, ask the Holy Spirit to help guide you in wisdom; you will be surprised at how much can be revealed by simply asking.

(NIV, 2 Samuel 22:3-4), *"My God is my rock, in whom I take refuge, my shield and the horn of my salvation. He is my stronghold, my refuge, and my Savior; from the violent people, You save me. I called to the Lord who is worthy of praise, and I have been saved from my enemies."*

You are protected on so many levels by your Heavenly Father. You can find refuge in Him, and rest assured that He will shield you and fight your battles against evil. How wonderful to know that you have a protector!

Last but certainly not least, (NIV, John 13:34), *"A new command I give you: Love one another. As I have loved you, so you must love one another."*

You are loved. The love of the Lord is so perfect, so whole, so complete, there isn't really a way we can comprehend it here on earth. We can say we love pizza, a favorite show, or a new pair of shoes, but nothing compares to the Lord's love for you. The Bible uses a special word for God's love, "Agape," which means self-sacrificing, unconditional love from one who always does what's best for the one they love.

When God sent His one and only Son to die for our sins so that we could have eternal life in Heaven with Him, this was one of the easiest ways to understand the Father's love for us. So, give yourself a hug and proclaim every day of your life, *I am loved.*

The next time you question your identity, remember who God says you are, and if you have to, start by listing everything you are not.

You are not your anxiety. You are not weak. You are not your depression. You are not your addiction. You are not out of control, alone, or abandoned. You are not worthless, despite how paralyzed you may feel from the storm you are experiencing. It is so very important, even though we may feel *all* of these negative labels of who we are, that we separate emotion from the truth and replace every negative label with the truth label our Savior gives us. Despite everything you may be feeling, you are strong and amazing and will get through this!

Proclaim:

- I am made in the image of God. –Genesis 1:27
- I was chosen by God long before my birth. I am not a mistake. –Jeremiah 1:5
- I am a child of God, the child of the mightiest King. –John 1:12
- I am an heir to all that God has. –Galatians 4:7
- I am blessed. –Ephesians 1:3
- The blessings of God overtake me. I can't outrun them. –Deuteronomy 28:2
- I am accepted. –Romans 5:12
- I am known. –Psalm 139:1-4
- I am forgiven. –Romans 8:1
- I am saved. –Romans 10:9-10
- I am free. –John 8:36
- I am able. –2 Corinthians 9:8
- I am smart. –James 1:5
- I am protected. –2 Samuel 22:3-4
- I am loved. –John 13:34

# CHAPTER 2: WHO IS GOD?

*"For I am the Lord your God, who takes hold of your right hand and says to you, 'Do not fear; I will help you.'"* –Isaiah 41:13 (NIV)

So now that we have a good base of who we are, who is God? Bible School will tell us He is the creator of the universe, which is true. Still, that title seems so far removed from the genuinely amazing being that He is, for He is so much more than the parameters we set for Him. (NIV, John 1:4-5) tells us, *"In Him was Life, and that Life was the light of all mankind. The Light shines in the darkness, and the darkness has not overcome it."*

So, what is light? The dictionary defines light as *"something that makes vision possible."* Without God, we cannot have spiritual vision. Spiritual vision allows us to see God's truth. How interesting that God's life gives vision to all humanity, not just vision that comes from a lightbulb, but real spiritual vision. Vision that allows us to see through the dark lies of the enemy. Vision that unveils the truth when the world surrounds us with deceit. Vision that darkness has never been able to overpower. How amazing that God thought enough about us to fill Himself with light and truth, so He could lead us through a victorious life. If we walk through life with God, we will know truth and never be overpowered by darkness. Praise God!

One of my favorite movies is *The Shack*, which tells the fictional story of a man whose young daughter was kidnapped and murdered, eventually leading him to confront God with his anger and hurt. In the movie, Mac, the father, receives a mysterious letter from someone asking to meet him at the cabin where the police presumed his daughter had been murdered (they never found her body). The letter was signed, "Papa," an endearing term that his wife called God. Mac had a lousy relationship with his father growing up and was furious with and distant from God over his daughter's death.

When Mac makes it to the cabin and meets God, God initially appears as a woman resembling the nanny he had as a child. As the movie progresses, the ending scenes show God as an older, stronger man. When Mac asks God why He has taken this different form, God replies, "I thought you could use a Father today."

Now, before you go crazy and start ranting that God should not be a woman because the Bible clearly states that God is our Father in Heaven, I want you to set aside all of the technicalities and just focus on the fundamental principle of the story. God knew what Mac needed, and what he needed at the beginning of his journey to the cabin was someone who resembled the most nurturing person he knew: a woman who took care of him when he was a child after his mother left him alone with his abusive father. Toward the end, God gave him a father because he was coming up against a very challenging moment where he needed the strength of a Father. Takeaway: God is everything we need at every moment of every day. He is a comforter when we need comforting; a healer when we need healing. He is a physician when we need a cure and direction when we are lost. He mends us when we are broken and shields us from the enemy's attacks.

In the words of Priscilla Shirer, *"He is everything for everybody, everywhere, every time and in every way. He is your God, and THAT is who you belong to."* You belong to a God Who has no limits. A God Who, with mere words, created the heavens and the earth. (NIV, Genesis 1:1-5), *"In the beginning, God created the heavens and the earth. Now the earth was formless and empty, and darkness was over the surface of the deep, and the Spirit of God was hovering over the waters. And God said, 'Let there be light,' and there was light. God saw that the light was good, and He separated the light from the darkness. God called the light 'Day,' and the darkness He called 'Night.' And there was evening, and there was morning – the first day."*

On God's first day of creation, He chose to separate light from the darkness. God knew how important it was to give darkness boundaries so it never again had the chance to overpower the light. We have a

God Who is concerned about our past, present, and future. He cares about us so much that He couldn't imagine a life without us, so He sent His only Son to die for us, to be the Sacrificial Lamb for our sins. (NIV, John 3:16), *"For God so loved the world that He gave His one and only Son, that whoever believes in Him shall not perish, but have eternal life."*

God meets us where we are, in the middle of our struggle. He isn't surprised by anything we present to Him. He cries with us when we are sad, and His heart breaks when ours does. (NIV, John 11:35), the shortest verse in the Bible, says *"Jesus wept."* Jesus had just gotten word that His dear friend Lazarus was dead. If you look deeper, you will see Jesus's connection to humanity. (NIV, John 11: 32-36), *"When Mary reached the place where Jesus was and saw Him, she fell at His feet and said, 'Lord, if You had been here, my brother would not have died.' When Jesus saw her weeping, and the Jews who had come along with her also weeping, He was deeply moved in spirit and troubled. 'Where have you laid him?' He asked. 'Come and see Lord,' they replied. Jesus wept. Then the Jews said, 'See how He loved him!'"*.

Jesus wept. When we are going through life and struggling, we are not alone. God sent Jesus as an earthly reminder that He connects and understands what we are going through on a human level. As we journey through this book, we will see that God has a complete set of armor to put on for protection (Ephesians 6:11). He sends angels to minister to us, and in our most depressed moments, He comforts us (1 Kings 19:5-7). He calms the storms around us (Mark 4:39). When we are trapped on every side, He will make a way for us through the deep waters that lie ahead (Exodus 14:21). (ESV, 2 Corinthians 1:3-4), *"Blessed be the God and Father of our Lord Jesus Christ, the Father of mercies, and God of all comfort, who comforts us in all our affliction, so that we may be able to comfort those who are in any affliction, with the comfort with which we ourselves are comforted by God."* God comforts us in ALL afflictions and strengthens us to comfort those around us with His same compassion and love. God took the form of Jesus, our best friend, confidant, and role model. He taught us how to pray (Matthew 6:9-13), and He taught us how to not judge those who seem to sin in a different way than we do (John 8:7).

God sent Jesus to show that He loves you despite your past; despite any embarrassment or mistakes, Jesus will reveal Himself to you, knowing all you have done but choosing to love you anyway. (John 4:4-26). When Jesus's time on earth expired, God sent the Holy Spirit to stay with us, live inside of us, and guide us as we journey back home to Him. (John 14:26). No matter what you are up against in life, God is there to meet your needs and be exactly who you need Him to be, every second of every day. In this book, we will encounter numerous examples of ordinary people met by an extraordinary God. A God Who never left, never abandoned, and, most importantly, never gave up on them. The first and greatest commandment is this, *"You shall love the Lord your God with all your heart, and with all your soul, and with all your mind."* (ESV, Matthew 22:37). This requires us to have a deep personal relationship with God.

In the pages to come, I hope the stories of those who have gone before will inspire you, guide you, and teach you how wonderful it is to have God on your side, no matter what life throws at you. (NIV, Hebrews 4:15), *"For we do not have a High Priest who is unable to empathize with our weakness, but we have One who has been tempted in every way, just as we are—yet He did not sin."* Who is God? He chose to understand what we are experiencing, not for His own benefit, but for ours. Quite simply, He is Love.

# CHAPTER 3: THANKFUL

*"If the only prayer you said in your whole life was, 'Thank You,' that would suffice."* –Meister Eckhart

Yes, you are going to think I am crazy. We are going to take a moment. Stop here and thank God for the panic, the anxiety, the addiction, the depression, and any other struggle you are going through. There are so many reasons why this is important, and we can't move forward in our healing without this first step. (NLT, 1 Thessalonians 5:18), *"Be thankful in ALL circumstances, for this is God's will for you, who belong to Christ Jesus."* It is easy to thank God when everything is going our way; it's quite another to thank God when the waters are murky and the storms of change, disappointment, and despair are circling around us.

Being thankful does not mean that you enjoy all things or are pleased or happy with the circumstances encompassing your life at every given moment. It simply means that you surrender the chaos of the situation to the Lord and thank Him for His greater plan that you cannot see yet.

The apostle Paul wrote two letters to the believers in Thessalonica, now included among his other letters as books in the New Testament. He was certainly no stranger to fear, turmoil, and chaos. Paul had been beaten, and over a five-year span, imprisoned, put under house arrest, and escorted by a Roman guard. Despite his unfavorable circumstances, he always remembered to stay thankful. While writing his letter to the church in Philippi, Paul was in prison, and although he was chained and uncertain of his future, he wrote these words:

*"I thank God every time I remember you. In all my prayers for all of you, I always pray with joy because of your partnership in the gospel from the first day until now, being confident, of this, that He who began a good work in you will carry it on to completion until the day of Jesus Christ. It is right for me to feel this way about all of you since I have you in my heart, and, whether I am in chains or defending and confirming the gospel, all of you share in God's grace with me. God can testify how I long for all of you with the affection of Christ Jesus." (NIV, Philippians 1:3-8)*

Wow. Just wow. Not only does Paul start giving thanks, but then he gives encouragement to the people of Philippi, despite his circumstance.

We can learn a lot from Paul and how he handled the very challenging moments of life. The book of Philippians is considered the happiest book in the Bible and was written from a Roman jail cell. Paul's message is this: we need to give thanks and get outside of ourselves. Often, during a struggle, we become so consumed with what's happening in us and around us that we trap ourselves further in our problems. One of the key components in conquering fear is keeping a good attitude and giving thanks. No matter what happens, give thanks. God can do much more with a heart full of thanks than with a bitter, closed-off heart consumed with fear and dread. In (NIV, Philippians 4:6), Paul writes, *"Do not be anxious about anything, but in every situation, by prayer and petition, with thanksgiving, present your requests to God."* Again, in the midst of uncertainty, Paul gives hope and assurance. This must have been a very challenging letter to write. I can't imagine Paul's fear during his imprisonment when he wasn't sure if he would make it through the night. To write this verse, he must have had incredible faith in God, the unwavering faith that we, too, can and will have.

There was a day when I was facing a lot of anxiety. I hadn't been to church in weeks because I couldn't get myself in the car and drive the hour round trip, fearing something terrible would happen. Some days I would get in the car, pull down the driveway, pull right back in, and watch the service online. I can't explain it, but my stomach would be in knots, I would feel dizzy and shaky, and my heart would start racing.

It was miserable, and I felt so defeated every time it happened. A lot of times, my daughter and I would both be in the car, and I would break down in tears and start crying, telling her how embarrassed and sorry I was that I couldn't go. I mentally and physically couldn't bring myself to go.

On this one particular Sunday, I woke up and got the two of us ready for church. I took anxiety medicine to help me relax and I was determined to make it to church. We got in the car; I checked my blood sugar (because that was my ultimate fear), and it was around 83 (which was a good number, but it still freaked me out), so I ate a half of a tuna sandwich and a cup of lentil soup on our way (more than enough food to sustain me). I was determined to go. During the entire ride, my heart was racing a million miles a minute, and I just kept saying, "satan, you have no power here" and "Jesus help me." I silently cried the entire way to the church. We showed up, and I retook my blood sugar (hoping it was at least 90-100 because of the food I ate), and lo and behold, it was at 81... it had dropped, even after the soup and sandwich, because of my panicking! My body was literally working against itself, my mind started racing, and I fell into a complete panic attack.

My daughter was so excited to put her five dollars in the offering box, and all I could think about was my blood sugar dropping and me possibly passing out. We quickly went in, found the offering box, and left out the back door. I brought my daughter back to the car, put the service on my phone, took out the other half of the tuna sandwich, and started sobbing. She held my hand as I once again expressed how sorry and embarrassed I was.

This wasn't me. A year ago, this wasn't me, yet here I was, a complete neurotic mess unable to do simple tasks. I felt so defeated, out of control, and alone. God? Where are you? I made it here, and I'm even more scared than when I started. What gives? I cried more on the way home, got in the door, crawled into bed, grabbed my Bible, and fell asleep saying the only thing I knew to say, "Thank you, God, today was terrible, I love you, I don't understand why I have to go through this, but thank you." I fell asleep and woke up feeling anxious but rested.

Sometimes we don't get an answer as to why things happen. We don't get the preview of knowing the purpose of our pain or why we go through the things we go through. Still, I can assure you that despite the circumstance, giving thanks no matter what is always a great first step. The enemy hates it when we are thankful after a traumatic or upsetting experience. His goal is to defeat us, and when we can walk away and still stay grateful for the challenge and the trial, we win. God wins.

I had a choice that day. I could have let myself fall into a depressed and defeated mental state. Instead, I chose to accept the emotion of fear that I was experiencing and thank God for all He had done, specifically for the trial He was walking me through, knowing that there would eventually be freedom on the other side. There is always power in a positive attitude and even more power when we give thanks.

Giving thanks allows God to work in unexpected ways. Looking back, I am very thankful for the panicked year I experienced. The strength that I gained, not just mentally but spiritually, is something that I will take with me on my life's journey. You will never regret the challenge that brings you closer to God.

# CHAPTER 4: PROWLING ABOUT

*"The enemy can be vicious, but he is not victorious."* –Lysa TerKeurst

So, I hate to be the bearer of bad news, but you have an enemy. I'm not talking about the snobby popular girl in school that always seemed to have it out for you or the guy at work that always tries to make you look bad in front of the boss. I'm talking about a downright evil, nasty, ruthless, lying, vindictive, manipulating force whose sole purpose is to destroy you. He has made it his job to study your every move and know exactly what buttons to push to throw you into a total mental panic; he has had a bullseye on you since birth, and the only way to escape him is to face him head-on, stand your ground and speak the only thing that he MUST listen to…the word of God.

The Bible says in (NIV, 1 Peter 5:8-9), *"Be alert and of sober mind. Your enemy, the devil prowls around like a roaring lion, looking for someone to devour. Resist him, standing firm in the faith, because you know that the family of believers throughout the world is undergoing the same kind of sufferings."* So, here are a few takeaways: 1) He prowls about like a *roaring* lion, so that's terrifying but also good because if he's roaring, then we can identify that he's coming. As scary as a roaring lion, I prefer that over a silent sniper attack. 2) The trick with the roar of the lion is to be so in tune with the Holy Spirit that you can hear when the attack is coming. Suppose we allow ourselves to be separated from God and our mental/spiritual bank account falls into the negative. In that case, we will have difficulty discerning when we are under attack.

We are often under attack and don't even realize it; we get so good at justifying sin that we accept the attack as part of our daily routine. When I was in high school, a youth minister shared this: "Satan doesn't want to knock you a full 180 degrees; he only wants to knock you off by one degree. Think of a circle with a dot in the middle. If you draw a line from the dot straight north and then draw a line just one degree to the right, as the lines are drawn farther and farther away, the space between the lines stays just far enough apart that you aren't one with God. You're close but just not there. This is how satan works. The degree he knocks you doesn't seem like much initially; however, a decision that bumps you one degree apart soon turns into another decision that bumps you another degree, and so on, and you don't even realize what is happening. Then, after years of traveling one degree off at a time, the distance from the initial line and the new line becomes so far apart that God can seem unreachable."

This always stuck with me as I ventured into adulthood. We always expect a big, bold attack that will rock our world, and honestly, sometimes, that's exactly how it happens. Still, other times, we only get knocked off course by a little, but that little bit after a long time creates a wide separation between you and God. Remember, satan's strongest attribute is that he is patient. He will plant a seed of doubt, fear, insecurity, etc., and he has no problem waiting years for the full-blown effect to take place. He is patient because he needs time for his plan to dig deep roots and take hold in our lives.

So, again, I am stressing the importance of knowing the word of God in and out so that when these tiny tactical seeds are placed in our minds, we can recognize and get rid of them before the roots have time to form and dig deep. Here are two examples of tiny, seemingly insignificant seeds planted that can wreck us over time:

1) You made a commitment to join a bible study on Monday nights. A few hours before the study starts, one of your friends messages you to go to happy hour. You justify that there will be other bible study nights, and it's OK to miss one, so you skip and chill with your friend. This seems harmless and justifiable, right? Wrong. There's a saying that goes, "If satan can't destroy you, he will distract you." This is so very important for us to grasp and understand. Satan takes something that seems harmless and uses it as a tiny wedge to

separate us from God. Suppose he throws enough wedges in our life that God becomes increasingly distant. Then satan doesn't have to try so hard anymore to break our relationship with our Savior. A good verse to help when these situations arise is (CEV, Matthew 5:37), *"When you make a promise, say only 'Yes or No.' Anything else comes from the devil."* God knew in advance that we would have trouble making decisions in the gray areas of life. Deep down, we all know the "right" decisions to make; however, the pressures of other people's opinions, what our flesh wants, and ultimately what God wants, all hinder how we respond and choose what to do.

2) You make a commitment to wake up and exercise every morning. You may start strong, but after a few weeks, you begin to feel like sleeping in ten minutes longer, or staying up a little later the night before, and suddenly you are too tired to work out the following day. There are a million and one excuses you come up with to slowly start putting off the commitment you used to be so excited about. You might say, "Well, this is about exercise. What does it have to do with God? So, what if I break a commitment to exercise, it won't affect me spiritually." (NIV, I Corinthians 6:19-20) tells us, *"Do you not know that your bodies are temples of the Holy Spirit, Who is in you, Whom you have received from God? You are not your own; You were bought at a price. Therefore, honor God with your bodies."* Exercising and staying healthy is one of the ways we can honor God, so we can't be surprised when satan comes after us by attacking our intentions of keeping ourselves healthy and strong. When we try to make ourselves the best version we can be, it angers our adversary, whose sole goal is to have us become the worst version of ourselves. He hates any progress we make. Brothers and sisters, this is why knowing the word of God is so important. We must know it so well that identifying an attack becomes second nature.

So, now that we know a few ways in which we can be distracted from the will of God by the adversary, we need to learn how to stand our ground and speak back to him, for he will not give up easily. This has become my favorite phrase to speak against satan's mental attacks: "Spirit of Fear, I bind you in the name of Jesus!" In the name of Jesus, we call on everything He is to send satan back to Hell and protect us from any fear we are being provoked to experience.

It is so wonderful to be able to call on the name of Jesus when we are afraid, panicked, or in trouble. You see, Jesus himself, being fully human and divine, also experienced attacks from the adversary. (NIV, Matthew 4:1-11), *"Then Jesus was led by the Spirit into the wilderness to be tempted by the devil. After fasting for forty days and forty nights, He was hungry. The tempter came to Him and said, 'If you are the Son of God, tell these stones to become bread.' Jesus answered, 'It is written, man shall not live on bread alone, but on every word that comes from the mouth of God.' Then the devil took Him to the holy city and had Him stand on the highest point of the temple. 'If you are the Son of God,' he said, 'throw yourself down. For it is written: He will command his angels concerning you, and they will lift You up in their hands, so that You will not strike Your foot against a stone.' Jesus answered him, 'It is also written: Do not put the Lord your God to the test.' Again, the devil took Him to a very high mountain and showed Him all the kingdoms of the world and their splendor. 'All this I will give You if You bow down and worship me.' Jesus said to him, 'Away from Me, satan! For it is written, Worship the Lord your God and serve Him only.' Then the devil left Him, and the angels came and attended Him."*

I find this passage in Matthew so intriguing. To get some context, Matthew chapter 3, verse 17 concludes with Jesus' baptism and the voice from Heaven declaring, *"Behold this is my Son, my beloved, in whom I delight!"* Immediately following that verse, we see that Jesus was led by the Holy Spirit into the wilderness to be tempted. Let's read that one more time…who led Jesus into the desert to be tempted? *The Holy Spirit!* As Christians, we tend to think that once we are "saved," life will go easy, and there may be some bumps, but for the most part, life will be good. Jesus is our prime example that this is not the case. Jesus was the Lord's beloved Son, with Whom He was well pleased, yet He still allowed the Holy Spirit to lead Him into the wilderness to be tested.

Often when we face the adversary, we feel like we do so alone because we must have done something terrible to deserve it. I am not saying that our poor choices don't bring on negative consequences; what I am saying is that sometimes, in order to do the will of God and in order to complete the mission He has for your life, this requires you to be tested, tempted, and tried by the devil, and the only One to lead you into the struggle is the Holy Spirit. How else will God know you are ready to carry out His specific mission for your life?

The good news is that if the Holy Spirit is leading you into dark waters to test your faith, you know you aren't alone. The Bible promises in (NIV, John 14:16), *"And I will ask the Father, and He will give you another advocate to help you and be with you forever."* Jesus promises that the Holy Spirit will be with us forever. So, no matter what anxious moments lie ahead, you are not alone, and if the Spirit leads you in, then the Spirit will guide you out.

At the end of Jesus's temptation in the wilderness, it says that the angels surrounded Him and ministered to Him. Jesus was tested and tried, but the angels were never far away to give Him relief. Another interesting takeaway from Matthew 4:1-11 is that satan chose to begin his attack when Jesus was hungry and tired. How many of us don't get enough sleep at night and are completely drained and not our "best" selves the next day, making silly mistakes and running on empty? Satan doesn't attack when we are completely rested and feeling great; he waits for a weak moment where he can get us in a vulnerable state.

The first thing Jesus was tempted with was food. How ironic, right? After forty days of fasting, that would be the most obvious thing Jesus would want. The second temptation from satan is a little more strategic. It truly shows the capacity of evil we are up against in our battles. Satan tempts Jesus to throw Himself down…but not from a random place. Satan brings Jesus to the Holy City and sets Him on the temple's highest point. Satan is strategic and purposeful. He chose a Holy City and a Holy Place to get Jesus to waver, then verbally followed up with, *"For it is written…"* Satan not only tempts Jesus, but he uses the written word of God to combat Him.

This should be eye-opening to every one of you going through a struggle. Satan flipped the script on Jesus during His second temptation and tried to confuse Him with the word of God and a Holy location. Jesus's first response to the first temptation was, *"For it is written…"* So satan decided to use the same wording in his next attack. It's as if he was trying to get Jesus to justify His decision to throw Himself down by using the word of God against Him. If Jesus were to throw Himself down from anywhere, it would probably feel most comfortable and safe for Him to do so in a Holy City on top of a Holy Temple. He would most likely feel that his Father was not far away to save Him from there.

Sometimes when going through a very intense spiritual struggle, it is pretty easy to confuse the word of God if we aren't being led by the Holy Spirit. Sometimes we can even get a thought in our head that "sounds good" but might not be what God wants. Prayer and constant conversation with God are beneficial in those challenging discerning moments.

The third and final time Jesus was tempted, He responded with, *"Away with you, Satan!"* and continued with, *"For it is written…"* Jesus had had quite enough and commanded Satan to leave. We also need to get to that point during our struggles. When is enough, enough? How much can you take before you are so completely done that you snap and can't take any more?

Jesus has been there, too, and when Jesus commands satan to leave, he must listen. After the angels ministered to Jesus, the Bible goes on in the following few verses to say that Jesus left Nazareth, went to Capernaum, and began preaching. Jesus had to be tested and pass the test before He could begin His ministry and eventually die so that we could all have eternal life.

How comforting is that! If you are going through the most intense struggle of your life, praise God! This means that He has an excellent plan for you, and you are in the stages of fine-tuning before being used entirely by your Heavenly Father. Jesus' testing in the wilderness didn't last forever, and neither will yours.

(ESV, John 10:10), *"The thief comes only to steal and kill and destroy, but I have come so that you may have life and life it abundantly."*

Satan has one agenda, and it's to take you out. There's a saying that goes, "If satan isn't bothering you, then there's a good chance you aren't doing anything to bother him." Scary thought. So, if you are going through the scariest, most anxious time of your life, and you feel like the attacks just aren't letting up, stay strong and find some peace knowing that you must be doing something pretty incredible for God if the devil is after you as hard as he is. It's been said that the devil only attacks what's important. If you are reading this book, then I can guarantee you are extremely important and valuable to God.

John 10:10 references satan as a thief coming to steal, kill and destroy. This doesn't always mean physically. Satan can steal your peace of mind. He can steal your joy, destroy your marriage, your relationship with your children, and your parents. Satan can kill dreams and ambitions, leaving you with feelings of despair. We must be vigilant in standing our ground against the adversary. (NLT, 1 Peter

5:9) tells us, *"Stand firm against him and be strong in your faith. Remember that your family of believers all over the world is going through the same kind of suffering you are."* The first area satan will attack is your mind. He knows that if he can weaken your thought process, he can control your actions, emotions, and beliefs. As much as satan is prowling about and ready to pounce at any moment, we must be one step ahead, always preparing ourselves in advance, meditating on the words and promises of God, having a constant conversation with God, and looking to the Holy Spirit for guidance. If we build ourselves up with the truth of the word, satan will have to get through quite the barrier to reach us.

You can make proclamations throughout your day to help keep you grounded in the word of God. Saying things like, "The devil is NOT going to deceive me anymore," or, "I cast down all wrong thoughts from the devil," help you take a positive claim over your life and help set some clear boundaries with the adversary on what you are willing and not willing to tolerate.

Let's take a look at King David for a minute. King David was a man after God's own heart, but if you read about his life, he made quite a few mistakes. In NIV, 2 Samuel chapter 11:1-27 below, we will look closer at King David and how his choices let satan sneak in and wreak chaos in his life. It's crucial that we read all 27 verses in order to get the context of what is going on and how easily we can be deceived by satan.

**David and Bathsheba**

1 *"In the spring, at the time when kings go off to war, David sent Joab out with the king's men and the whole Israelite army. They destroyed the Ammonites and besieged Rabbah. But David remained in Jerusalem.*

2 *One evening David got up from his bed and walked around on the roof of the palace. From the roof he saw a woman bathing. The woman was very beautiful,* 3 *and David sent someone to find out about her. The man said, 'She is Bathsheba, the daughter of Eliam and the wife of Uriah the Hittite.'* 4 *Then David sent messengers to get her. She came to him, and he slept with her. (Now she was purifying herself from her monthly uncleanness.) Then she went back home.* 5 *The woman conceived and sent word to David, saying, "I am pregnant."*

6 *So David sent this word to Joab: 'Send me Uriah the Hittite.' And Joab sent him to David.* 7 *When Uriah came to him, David asked him how Joab was, how the soldiers were and how the war was going.* 8 *Then David said to Uriah, "Go*

*down to your house and wash your feet." So, Uriah left the palace, and a gift from the king was sent after him. [9] But Uriah slept at the entrance to the palace with all his master's servants and did not go down to his house.*

*[10] David was told, 'Uriah did not go home.' So, he asked Uriah, 'Haven't you just come from a military campaign? Why didn't you go home?'*

*[11] Uriah said to David, 'The ark and Israel and Judah are staying in tents,[a] and my commander Joab and my lord's men are camped in the open country. How could I go to my house to eat and drink and make love to my wife? As surely as you live, I will not do such a thing!'*

*[12] Then David said to him, 'Stay here one more day, and tomorrow I will send you back.' So Uriah remained in Jerusalem that day and the next. [13] At David's invitation, he ate and drank with him, and David made him drunk. But in the evening Uriah went out to sleep on his mat among his master's servants; he did not go home.*

*[14] In the morning David wrote a letter to Joab and sent it with Uriah. [15] In it he wrote, 'Put Uriah out in front where the fighting is fiercest. Then withdraw from him so he will be struck down and die.'*

*[16] So while Joab had the city under siege, he put Uriah at a place where he knew the strongest defenders were. [17] When the men of the city came out and fought against Joab, some of the men in David's army fell; moreover, Uriah the Hittite died.*

*[18] Joab sent David a full account of the battle. [19] He instructed the messenger: 'When you have finished giving the king this account of the battle, [20] the king's anger may flare up, and he may ask you, Why did you get so close to the city to fight? Didn't you know they would shoot arrows from the wall? [21] Who killed Abimelek son of Jerub-Besheth[b]? Didn't a woman drop an upper millstone on him from the wall, so that he died in Thebez? Why did you get so close to the wall?' If he asks you this, then say to him, 'Moreover, your servant Uriah the Hittite is dead.'*

*[22] The messenger set out, and when he arrived, he told David everything Joab had sent him to say. [23] The messenger said to David, 'The men overpowered us and came out against us in the open, but we drove them back to the entrance of the city gate. [24] Then the archers shot arrows at your servants from the wall, and some of the king's men died. Moreover, your servant Uriah the Hittite is dead.'*

*[25] David told the messenger, 'Say this to Joab: 'Don't let this upset you; the sword devours one as well as another. Press the attack against the city and destroy it. Say this to encourage Joab.'*

*[26] When Uriah's wife heard that her husband was dead, she mourned for him. [27] After the time of mourning was over, David had her brought to his house, and she became his wife and bore him a son. But the thing David had done*

*displeased the Lord."*

So, that's a LOT. Let's break it down and see where David went wrong. For starters, David was supposed to be off at war. My pastor once said that if David had been doing what he was supposed to be doing, then satan wouldn't have had an opportunity to take a foothold in his life. Let's play it out—if David was off at war, he wouldn't have seen Bathsheba, he wouldn't have slept with her, gotten her pregnant, and he wouldn't have tried to get her husband Uriah to sleep with her to cover up his sin.

Further, when that plan failed, he wouldn't have sent Uriah to the front lines to be killed to hide the scandal, and he wouldn't have married Bathsheba. Now let's go over what David really did. David, for whatever reason, did not go off to war with his men as all the other kings did. This left him idle and with free, unaccounted-for time. How many of us can attest that we tend to get into trouble when we are left with idle time? There is a saying that goes, "Idle time is the devil's playground." We can get lazy in our walk with God which then transfers to laziness at work, in relationships, our appearance, and eating habits.

Idleness is not something to be taken lightly. Instead of being occupied with war, David was left with idle time, which was summed up so perfectly by my wonderful pastor, "it led David to be where he wasn't supposed to be, see something he wasn't supposed to see, and do something he wasn't supposed to do."

David's choices led to Uriah's death and God's disappointment. See how quickly satan can sneak in and attack even the Godliest of men? All it took was for David to let down his guard. The fantastic news here is that God still called David "A man after His own heart." God still had Jesus come from David's lineage and loved David because, despite everything, God knew David's heart.

So, if you feel like you have had times in your life where you can relate to David, ask your heavenly Father for forgiveness and move on. Holding onto your sin only gives the adversary leverage to hold guilt over you, and no one needs that! Satan is a liar and a deceiver, only looking to steal, kill, and destroy, for he prowls around like a roaring lion, looking for someone to devour. It is so important that you are purposeful in what you are supposed to be doing in your day-to-day life so that you don't give satan an opportunity to get a foothold.

# CHAPTER 5: PRISON OF YOUR MIND

*"It all begins and ends with your mind. What you give power to, has power over you, if you allow it."* –Leon Brown

For lack of better words, the prison of your mind is "the scary place." It's like the fun house of mirrors, and everywhere you turn, you run into yourself over and over and over again. You try to push through but only end up pushing up against mirrored walls showing images of YOU literally in your own way. Your head starts to spin, breathing becomes labored, and your heart races as you scramble to find a way out. Hands clenched, sweat pouring, you frantically push around at all the glass walls, hoping and praying that the end is near, and you can be free. All the while, your fear is building up more and more in your mind, digging deeper and deeper into your memory. Your brain starts to run with terrible scenarios of your deepest fear until you are almost entirely consumed with every possible dreaded ending.

You go through this feeling any time a negative thought takes hold. It could be a medical, relational, work, financial, or even an irrational fear. Regardless of the fear, the entrapment is real. The feelings and emotions are real, and the escape seems unattainable. You are trapped inside yourself, and the sudden sinking feeling sets in that you will *never* be able to leave yourself. It's the one place you can't escape. Ever. No matter how hard you try, you will never be able to escape yourself and live a normal life. You become depressed as you start thinking of your future, asking yourself questions like *How am I ever going to attend this event, or go on this vacation, or purchase this, or send my children to this college, or lose weight, or find my soul mate?* The thoughts of the future pile up and, one by one, weigh you down, pushing you further and further into the scary place of your mind.

You may try to escape with alcohol, drugs, poor moral choices, etc., but the fact remains when all is said and done, the Band-aids don't help. The fear is still there, worse than before. Every futile attempt to escape has been tried. You are NEVER getting out. The thought sinks in deeper as you go through your daily routine of making breakfast, preparing lunches, helping kids with homework, and meeting clients.

You barely make it through most days, crying intermittently and feeling completely mentally exhausted by early afternoon. Getting through the day is a task you complete by the skin of your teeth, and you have nothing left to give by the time you get home. You try to sleep, but the fears that consumed your day creep into your dreams, or should I say nightmares. You toss and turn all night as your deepest fears re-present themselves while your body tries to rest and recuperate for the next day.

My aunt used to say, "It's the brain that needs rest, not the body," and boy, was she right! No matter how much sleep you get, if your brain doesn't rest, your emotions and feelings are much worse the following day. This pattern continues until you're reduced to doing only the bare minimum; the simple tasks you once took pleasure in are now looming chores that seems daunting to achieve…so you then ask yourself why bother trying?

Work suffers, relationships suffer, your health suffers, and finances suffer as you scramble to reclaim any sort of 'normal' back into your life. Does any of this sound familiar? I lived this for a long time. A *very* long time. The feeling of being trapped in your mind, where you not only manifest your fear but then keep yourself stuck in the horror of it on repeat, is an extremely terrifying place to be. You wake up with the fear, are constantly reminded of the fear throughout the day, fall asleep with the fear, you dream about the fear, and repeat.

If you have been here or are here now, take a breath, it's OK because if I could reclaim my mind, so can you. So now what? The Bible reassures us that although we can feel all these things, we have a God who is greater, a God who is a deliverer, and a Savior from all of our suffering. Praise God!

In ESV, Matthew 6:9-13, Jesus gives us the perfect way to pray:

*"Pray then like this: 'Our Father in heaven, hallowed (holy) be your name. Your kingdom come, Your will be done, on earth as it is in heaven. Give us this day our daily bread, and forgive us our debts, as we also have forgiven our debtors. And lead us not into temptation, but deliver us from evil.'"*

In verse 11, Jesus specifically says, *"Give us THIS DAY our daily bread."* One might argue that we could break that down even more and say give us this moment, this second, this hour. Lord, give me enough to sustain this moment because I am scared and can't do this without You. Jesus knew that we would never be enough on our own to make it through even one day without Him. He is purposeful, and there is no doubt in my mind that He specifically placed verse 11 as a simple reminder to rely on God for all our needs. We must believe, truly believe, that what we ask for in prayer He will fulfill; He will help sustain us and bring us through to victory.

Prayer and speaking back to satan's lies will be our greatest weapon in escaping the prison of our mind. (NKJV, 2 Timothy 1:7), *"For God has not given us a spirit of fear, but of power, and of love and of a sound mind."*

God prepared us with the tools we would need to defeat the enemy, but just like any good weapon, we must practice with it until it becomes second nature. We were given power and a sound mind. Hooray! That means that the "scary place," the mirror maze we get trapped in without escape, is a façade.

Picture it as the foyer of the mind. We get there first, and instead of knowing and claiming everything we know God created us to be, we get trapped in the scary, the panic, and the anxious thoughts before we even step through the door to the actual house where the true thoughts of the mind reside. So how do we tear down this scary foyer and rebuild a grand entrance full of hope, love, and peace? It's going to take a lot of work. A LOT OF WORK. This is not going to be a task for the faint of heart. This is going to be arguably the hardest battle of your life. You will have to face your fears, yourself, and your greatest enemy all at once.

Consider it the final battle to win the kingdom back. You will need to be purposeful, strategic, resilient, determined, and above all else, steadfast in the word of God, proclaiming ALL He is when everything inside and around you says otherwise. The devil will not give up easily. I would be lying to you if I said this was a quick fix. It's not. This is a battle, which means that *both sides* are prepared to fight and stand their ground. This will take time and will be draining; sometimes, you will retreat, and sometimes, you will find the strength to stand your ground, but the key is to never give up.

In the words of Sir Winston Churchill, "If you're going through Hell, keep going." This is how it's going to feel some days. You will fight your whole day and feel like you haven't made progress because that's precisely what the enemy wants you to think. I promise if you stand your ground, you will win. Remember, you don't drown by falling in a river; you drown by staying in it. So, let's make up our minds to not stay in the river. We will get ourselves out, and even if we're soaking wet and trembling, we will hold our heads high, stand our ground, stubbornly pressing on. For no one can defeat a child of God!

Now let's look at some strategies that will help you win this war and get that scary place in your mind re-conquered and given back to the authority of the rightful King.

So where do these negative thoughts come from? Picture, if you will, a person sitting on a park bench. They are just sitting there minding their own business when someone (they can't see but only hear) walks up behind them and starts whispering things like, "I bet you're going to get in a car accident today. You probably shouldn't drive. Did you even get your car serviced last month like you were supposed to? I bet the brakes aren't working right. A deer jumped out and hit your friend's car the other day. Luckily, they were OK, but I don't think you would be so lucky. Many people drive distracted nowadays, and I bet one will hit you on your way home, or worse, hit the side of the car your child is on, and your child might not make it."

Could you imagine the initial thought of the person on the bench? It might be something like this—*Nah, I'll be fine.* And then the next whisper comes, and the next whisper comes, and soon the person on the bench starts to consider the whispers and gives them a little more attention. Before they know it, the person on the bench begins to get anxious over driving for fear that something terrible might happen to them or their loved ones. The fear starts to grow and paralyzes them with indecisiveness.

This, brothers and sisters, is how satan works. Part of his prowling about is whispering nonsense into our minds. It doesn't take much, just a thought here, a whisper there, and if we aren't vigilant in protecting our mind and taking account of the ideas that go in and out, we are going to quickly be subjected to the lies and seeds planted by our enemy. (NIV, 2 Corinthians 10:5), *"We demolish arguments and every pretension that sets itself up against the knowledge of God, and we take captive every thought and make it obedient to Christ."*

The knowledge of God is truth, and satan is the father of lies. Anything that comes against what we know to be true, we need to shut down, capture it, and speak verses of life back into the situation to make the lie obedient to what the word of God says. Remember, satan is strategic and patient, so a tiny whisper of a thought today might not mean something. Still, a hundred small whispers of similar damaging thoughts over the course of a few weeks could lead to some devastating anxious and panicked moments down the road. It is crucial that we catch these thoughts at the onset so we can successfully fulfill the will of God and live the joyful life we were designed to live. So, what do we do? We take captive every negative thought and replace it with a good thought. We speak back to the negative thoughts and take control of the lies we are being told. Just because a thought enters your mind does not mean you are required to entertain it.

So how would the person on the park bench respond successfully to the negative whispers coming at them? At the onset of the *very first* whisper, the person would say, "No! I am not going to listen to this today. I know God is with me wherever I go and sends His angels to protect me and my family. I refuse to worry about something that hasn't happened, and I choose to trust God over this fear that you are trying to place in my mind. Leave me alone!"

We have power in our words. (ESV, Deuteronomy 28:7) says, *"The Lord will cause your enemies who rise up against you to be defeated before you. They shall come out against you one way and flee before you seven ways."* What a wonderful word from God! No matter what comes our way, God is on our side, which means that as the enemy inevitably rises up against us, ESPECIALLY when we start to break free from his lies and deception, we can have comfort knowing that for every attack that comes our way, he has to flee from us seven different ways, because Christ is in us. Proclaim, "satan, you have NO power here!"

What helped me a lot during the intense moments of panic was making a small stack of index cards that I could carry around. These cards stated proclamations against satan, speaking truth over the lies that were consuming me. I found it overwhelming to try and remember key verses and phrases off the top of my head as I battled to re-claim my mind, so these were especially helpful. A copy of the full set I used can be purchased online, but here are some key phrases to get you started:

- My mind is renewed every day by God.
- Satan, leave my mind; you are trespassing on God's anointed property!
- God, in this moment, I rest in You and You alone, no matter how anxious I am right now.
- The devil is NOT going to deceive me anymore.
- I cast down ALL wrong thoughts from the devil.
- I will not give in to this fear.
- This feeling is not going to last forever.
- The power of Almighty God is in this moment.
- God is in control; therefore, I am in control.
- Nothing can control me except the Holy Spirit.
- If God is for me, who can be against me?
- I cannot be defeated. The favor of God is on my life.
- Lord, Save me.
- Lord, Help me.
- "I will not be shaken!" –Psalm 16:8
- Jesus speaks peace over my life every second of every day.
- "I sought the Lord, and he answered me and delivered me from ALL my fears." –Psalm 34:4
- The same power that raised Jesus from the dead lives in me; therefore, satan, you HAVE to listen to me when I tell you to leave.
- My heavenly Father is on his way! You picked the wrong person to mess with today!

I wouldn't recommend doing this in a public setting; however, I'm going to level with you and say that sometimes you must get downright angry with the adversary. I have literally been known to sit in my car, windows rolled up, and scream—literally scream—at satan. I have said things like, "GET THE HELL OUT OF MY MIND, LEAVE ME ALONE! YOU HAVE NO POWER HERE! YOU ARE TRESPASSING ON GOD'S ANOINTED PROPERTY! IN THE NAME OF JESUS, YOU HAVE TO LEAVE! THE SAME POWER

THAT RAISED CHRIST FROM THE DEAD LIVES IN ME, AND I COMMAND YOU TO GO!"

I know it sounds crazy, but so is having an irrational panic attack…so, I am only telling you this because it works. Satan is a bully; he throws his weight around and intimidates to the ultimate degree. If you want to win, FIGHT BACK. You can't do everything you have been doing thus far and expect a different result (the definition of true insanity). We are here to break bonds and chains and reclaim a new life in Christ. A life free from anxiety, panic, addiction, and depression.

So, get angry! Use your voice and shout back at the evil one who finds every joy in hurting you, stealing from you, and wreaking havoc on your mind. He delights in your worry, in your distress, and in your panicked all-night pacing.

Take all that anger, the anger of missing your children's performance because you were panicking in the parking lot, the anger of a divorce, the anger of financial distress, the anger of having to start your life over yet again, and the anger of addiction taking priority over your family's needs. Take all that anger and focus it back on the only entity that deserves to have it thrown right back in his face. Stand your ground. Proclaim the word of God and FIGHT.

# CHAPTER 6: EN GARDE

*"When one takes on the armor of God, Fear retreats into the shadows."*
–Brad Wilcox

So how do we prevent the attack from the enemy and fight successfully? It sounds completely exhausting always being alert. (NIV, Ephesians 4:27) says, *"Do not give the devil a foothold."* When we go about our daily lives and leave God out of the equation, we open ourselves up for the devil to take a foothold. We must be vigilant in protecting ourselves, renewing our minds every day in order to combat attacks from the adversary.

In fencing, "En Garde" means "Taking the opening position for action." This phrase is spoken by the referee right before the fight begins, alerting both players to get into position. What is the "En Garde" position for our spiritual life?

Our En Garde position needs to start before we even have an inkling that there will ever be a battle. It begins with a daily choice to consciously suit up with the armor of God. Ephesians 6:10-18 (NIV) says, *"Finally, be strong in the Lord and in His mighty power. Put on the full armor of God, so that you can take your stand against the devil's schemes. For our struggle is not against flesh and blood, but against the rulers, against the authorities, against the powers of this dark world, and against the spiritual forces of evil in the heavenly realms. Therefore, put on the full armor of God so that <u>when</u> the day of evil comes, you may be able to stand your ground and after you have done everything to stand. Stand firm then, with the belt of truth buckled around your waist, with* *the breastplate of righteousness in place, and with your feet fitted with the readiness that comes from the gospel of peace. In addition to all this, take up the shield of faith, with which you can extinguish all the flaming arrows of the evil one. Take the helmet of salvation and the sword of the Spirit, which is the word of God. And pray in the Spirit on all occasions with all kinds of prayers and requests. With this in mind, be alert and always keep on praying for all the Lord's people."*

Armor of God:

1) Belt of Truth
2) Breastplate of Righteousness
3) Shoes of Peace
4) Shield of Faith
5) Helmet of Salvation
6) Sword of the Spirit
7) Pray

It's interesting that Paul starts with the Belt of Truth. Back in Roman times, the belt held the sword, which allowed the soldier to have the ability to fight at any moment. We don't necessarily all use belts today; however, spiritually, we need the belt of truth. The belt of truth holds the sword of the spirit, which is the word of God that comes out of our mouths.

If we are in a spiritual battle, the word of God needs to be spoken back to the enemy through the filter of God's truth. Everything we say should be filtered through God's truth, so our words can have every effectiveness of the sharpest sword against the adversary.

The breastplate of righteousness is a piece that is supposed to protect our vital organs. Living in righteousness means that we live in the way God instructs us. We submit to His word and follow His ways. When we put on the breastplate of righteousness, we are covering our heart, which should forgive and love as the Lord instructs, and our lungs, which should carry every breath to praise God.

The shoes of peace prepare us to share the Gospel (Good News of Christ) with others everywhere we walk and wherever we go. This means that in all circumstances, we are prepared to respond as Jesus instructed to show others what it truly means to be a Christian.

The shield of faith is essentially the spiritual shield you set in front of yourself to block the adversary from all of his ongoing attacks. The shield of faith is important because, for it to function, it has to be raised up. Faith doesn't work unless you exercise it. You must be vigilant in keeping your faith strong so that the moment an attack begins, your shield is in position and ready. When you lift up every ounce of faith you have, your Father will keep you protected from the evil one.

The helmet of salvation is a very crucial piece of armor. The helmet clearly protects the head, where satan attacks us the hardest and strongest. Spiritual warfare in the form of a mental attack is satan's specialty. The doubts, negative thoughts, worries, and anxieties all enter the mind. The helmet of salvation needs to be firmly placed on the head and never removed, always focusing on God and the good that He has done.

There is a scene in *Saving Private Ryan* where a soldier is hit in the helmet with a bullet. He removes his helmet to inspect the hard impact. When his helmet is removed, an enemy soldier sees the opportunity and immediately shoots, killing him instantly. We have already discussed how satan prowls about, looking for every opportunity to attack. Suppose the helmet of salvation isn't securely put on and tightened. In that case, we are leaving ourselves wide open for one of satan's fatal attacks.

Finally, brothers and sisters, pray. We must pray with everything we have in order to fully protect ourselves against the attacks of the enemy. Prayer should be our first defense, not our last resort. At the onset of any problem, pray. As soon as you start to feel anxiety creeping up, pray. When you start feeling overwhelmed and don't know what to do, pray. Our prayers can open doors that no man can shut. Our constant conversation with God and releasing our prayers to Him allows Him to take action on our behalf, so suit up with your armor and PRAY. Stand your ground and PRAY. The full armor of God does not include armor for the backside of your body. This means that we don't run. We don't retreat in fear. So, stand firm in the strength we know God has surrounded us with and PRAY.

(NIV, Romans 8:26) tells us, *"We do not know what we ought to pray for, but the Spirit Himself intercedes for us through wordless groans."* The Holy Spirit is amazing! When we don't even know what to say, the Holy Spirit does and will intercede (intervene on our behalf, to the Father) and say the words we can't even find in our moment of distress. How absolutely incredible and comforting! When you are struggling, panicked, and full of anxiety, having no words left, the Holy Spirit is there to take over and handle the situation. This means that your tears are a prayer, your hurt in silence is a prayer, and your shaking, trembling, and nervous pacing are a prayer. Thank God that He loves us enough to send us an advocate to speak on our behalf when the weight of the world is too heavy to bear!

Just as the Holy Spirit is there for us, it is super important to build up a community of believers to surround us, pray with and for us, and speak life to our situation when we feel like we can't. A pastor once said, "Surround yourself with friends that call satan out on his lies when you are too tired and too confused to discern. He won't just have to take you out; now he will have to take you and the six of them out." What a powerful visual. It will be a tough and lonely battle if you are trying to fight and prepare on your own. How powerful is the thought of an army of believers surrounding you, holding you up, and going to battle with you!

Start taking inventory of who you keep in your close inner circle. Are they speaking life or death into the situations you face? Jesus tells us in NIV, Matthew 18:20, *"For where two or three gather in my name, there I am with them."* Jesus knew the importance of community in our battle against satan. If He is there when two or three gather, satan will have an impossible time taking everyone out. So, find a community, some faith-filled friends, and prepare your army. Proclaim, "I cannot be defeated if God is on my side! With the Holy Spirit as my constant helper, I will face and defeat the enemy every time he comes against me!"

# CHAPTER 7: WEAK DAYS

*"Give God your weakness, and He will give you His strength."*
--Captain Dale Black

There will be days when you feel like simply giving up. Days when enough is enough, you can't take it anymore. The burden of your anxiety, addiction and depression is too heavy to bear for one more second, the panic is relentless, and you can barely breathe. On these days, and in these moments, you have to muster up the very little strength you have left and declare one more time, "I am a child of God, and I will NOT be defeated."

Weak days are hard. I have had my fair share, and I'm going to be completely honest, they downright suck. These days are full of mostly sadness, tears, and depression; nothing makes you happy, and you have little hope for tomorrow. If and when you encounter a weak day, just remember you are not alone. Elijah had a weak day and was one of the greatest prophets in the Old Testament. He was so great he even performed many miracles!

To get a quick glimpse of Elijah's life, he raised a dead boy to life, stood up against 450 prophets of Baal and 400 prophets of Asherah, and called down fire from Heaven to prove that God was the One true God. He defeated all the Baal prophets. He was definitely a force to be reckoned with! However, like you and I, Elijah had a weak day. After he had defeated all of the Baal prophets, he got word from Jezebel, which can be found in 1 Kings 19:1-9 (NIV):

*1 "Now Ahab told Jezebel everything Elijah had done and how he had killed all*
*the prophets with the sword. 2 So Jezebel sent a messenger to Elijah to say, 'May*
*the gods deal with me, be it ever so severely if by this time tomorrow, I do not make*
*your life like that of one of them.'*

*3 Elijah was afraid and ran for his life. When he came to Beersheba in Judah,*
*he left his servant there, 4 while he himself went a day's journey into the wilderness.*
*He came to a broom bush, sat down under it and prayed that he might die. 'I have*
*had enough, Lord,' he said. 'Take my life; I am no better than my*
*ancestors.' 5 Then he lay down under the bush and fell asleep.*

*All at once an angel touched him and said, 'Get up and eat.' 6 He looked*
*around, and there by his head was some bread baked over hot coals, and a jar of*
*water. He ate and drank and then lay down again.*

*7 The angel of the Lord came back a second time and touched him and said,*
*'Get up and eat, for the journey is too much for you.' 8 So he got up and ate and*
*drank. Strengthened by that food, he traveled forty days and forty nights until he*
*reached Horeb, the mountain of God. 9 There he went into a cave and spent the*
*night."*

God's favor was certainly on Elijah, yet when he was threatened by one woman, he immediately came unraveled and prayed to die. How comforting to know that even the great prophet Elijah had a weak day! What I love about these verses is God's response. He sent an angel to minister to Elijah, and God did this not once but twice! Elijah was having a *really* weak day apparently! I love that God understood exactly where Elijah was coming from and sent what he needed to feel better. God knew Elijah's fleeting moment of weakness was not his true character, and He didn't hold it against him.

So, no matter what you are going through or how weak you may feel, please know it is temporary. Remember that you are in great company because even the great prophet Elijah felt the same way.

So how do we make it through our weak days? We speak life into a situation that seems hopeless. Robert Schuller once said, "Yard by yard life is hard; inch by inch, life's a cinch." That's a great motto for the weak days. We must take them inch by inch, make our way through them, and constantly remind ourselves that this will pass. On days I feel like I will not make it through, I constantly say, "God is my strength, *especially* on my weak days." It is so important that we remind ourselves that we don't have to rely on our own strength and that we have a Savior who is more than willing to take our burdens as His own and lighten our loads. *"Cast your burden on the Lord and He will sustain you."* (Psalm 55:22 ESV). Thank goodness we don't have to carry the weight of them alone!

I find myself speaking back to my hopeless thoughts by saying, "Satan give up because I refuse to give in." Even when I feel seconds from completely giving up, I continue to speak strength and hope into the situation. Remember that every testimony begins with a test, and we only grow on our most challenging days, for those are the days that build character and endurance. Proclaim that God is working everything out for your good. Believe that God is working on you and helping you no matter how you feel or how the situation may look. State with all certainty that God is preparing your breakthrough NOW! Remember, you will not FEEL strong on your weak days, and that's OK because God will be your strength. You need to focus on making it through, inch by inch, minute by minute. Philippians 4:19 (NIV) says, *"And my God will meet all your needs according to the riches of His glory in Christ Jesus."* How wonderful is that? Anything we need, God will provide, and that includes sustaining you on your weak days! Praise God!

So, remember, your job on these days is to speak life and rely on God to handle the rest. He already knew that you would need His help, and Psalm 46:1 (ESV) tells us, *"God is our refuge and strength, a VERY present help in trouble."* He isn't just "kinda" there when we need Him. The Bible tells us He is a VERY PRESENT help, which means He is on constant standby for any difficulty that comes our way. How wonderful to have that loving of a God!

One of my favorite quotes is from the movie Rocky V. "You, me or nobody is going to hit as hard as life. But it ain't about how hard you're hit. It's about how hard you can get hit and keep moving forward. How much you can take and keep moving forward. That's how winning is done!" Satan will hit hard and do it relentlessly. Remember, he literally has nothing better to do than destroy you. He doesn't care about rules or fair play. He will continually beat you until you can't take it anymore. You remind yourself that you are on the winning team because of Jesus' sacrifice. We already know how it all ends. So, muster up the little strength you have, and remind yourself that you are strong because Christ is strong. He lives in you. Refuse to be defeated by the heaviness of the weak days because, so far, your success rate for surviving them is 100%. So, Keep. Moving. Forward. You got this!

# CHAPTER 8: STORMS

*"Don't tell your God how big your storm is; tell your storm how big your God is."* –Unknown

Not every storm is in the forecast. Just like the weather, some storms are predicted, allowing us to prepare and protect ourselves and our belongings. Then every once in a while, a storm will turn up with little or no warning, bringing horrific winds, devastating rain, hail, and tornadoes. These storms leave you with little time to prepare and leave you and your belongings in a dangerous predicament. Storms like these come out of nowhere and only happen when conditions are "just right," like when warm and cold fronts collide.

How ironic that when two fronts collide is when we see these extremely damaging effects. Much like when we have a spiritual collision in our own lives, we see storms of a spiritual nature show up. Typically, we get slammed with an attack from the enemy when we are trying to progress in a direction other than God wants us to go. These moments can be terrifying and paralyzing. It could be the sudden loss of a job, death of a family member, illness, divorce, betrayal, or an irrational fear that grips your entire being and refuses to let go.

There are so many different "storms," but only one way to survive them; by anchoring your faith in Jesus. He is the ultimate Savior and will rebuke anything that comes your way. Remember, He is an EVER-PRESENT help in our time of need. A few times, I was blindsided by one of these storms from the enemy, and almost every time, it was when I was trying to "level up" in my spiritual life. Satan HATES it when we make spiritual progress. God loves giving us challenges to grow in our walk with Him, resulting in an unexpected life-threatening, damaging storm. (Yay!) These storms test our faith, our spiritual strength, our endurance, and most importantly, how much we trust God. The disciples experienced one of these storms, and we can learn a lot from how they responded.

*(NIV, Mark 4:35-41):* 35 *"That day when evening came, He said to His disciples, 'Let us go over to the other side'* 36 *Leaving the crowd behind, they took Him along, just as He was, in the boat. There were also other boats with Him.* 37 *A furious squall came up, and the waves broke over the boat so that it was nearly swamped.* 38 *Jesus was in the stern, sleeping on a cushion. The disciples woke Him and said to Him, 'Teacher, don't you care if we drown?'*

39 *He got up, rebuked the wind, and said to the waves, 'Quiet! Be still!' Then the wind died down and it was completely calm.*

40 *He said to His disciples, 'Why are you so afraid? Do you still have no faith?'*

41 *They were terrified and asked each other, 'Who is this? Even the wind and the waves obey him!'"*

To get some context, before the disciples were on the boat, they had spent much time with Jesus, witnessing Him perform miracle after miracle, speaking in parables, and teaching to large gatherings of people. They must have been so on fire for God after seeing firsthand all the incredible works He did. Could you imagine being there to see a leper healed in front of your very own eyes? Or a paralyzed man get up and walk?! They must have felt untouchable following Jesus around.

Now at the end of the day, they all got in the boat at Jesus' command and started to make their way across the Sea of Galilee. Jesus, in the stern of the boat, was sleeping on a cushion. Let's pause here for a minute. The stern of the boat is the very back of the boat, which means that if you were sitting in the stern, you probably wouldn't have the best view of what was coming your way. You would be removed from anything happening elsewhere on the boat. The rest of the disciples were on the main parts of the boat when the Bible says, *"A furious squall came up."* This was undoubtedly an unexpected storm for the disciples! The Bible continues to say, *"The waves broke over the boat so that it was nearly swamped."* We must remember that biblical scholars believe seven of the twelve disciples were fishermen, which means that they likely had experience handling a boat in less than favorable weather conditions. However, they panicked. Seven of the twelve were professional watermen, and they completely lost it when the storm arose.

When going about our business, we often don't prepare for a storm of this magnitude to come our way. The disciples were so consumed with everything they had experienced they let their guard down and were left vulnerable to satan's attacks. Even if we are very confident in a particular skill or area of our life, we can be deceived and made to feel like we can no longer employ that skill.

Satan is the father of lies and loves attacking our confidence. The disciples rush to Jesus, sleeping on a pillow, entirely at rest. They wake Him up and say, "Teacher, don't you care if we drown?!" Jesus gets up and rebukes the wind and the waves, saying, "Quiet! Be Still!" The storm immediately stops. An important note here is that Jesus, throughout the Bible, rebukes demons. He doesn't rebuke weather. The storm was sent as a distraction to unravel the disciples' faith. Jesus then turns to the disciples and says, "Why are you so afraid? Do you still have no faith?" Jesus was so close to the Father that He could rest peacefully amid the storm. The disciples forgot one key element—if Jesus was on the boat, then the boat wasn't going to sink. After experiencing and witnessing the miraculous works of Jesus, they still feared that He wouldn't help them.

We need to learn from their example and know without a shadow of a doubt that no matter what storm we face, no matter what comes our way, Jesus lives in us. He is Emmanuel (God in us, God with us, and God for us). There is NOTHING that will come our way that He can't give us the peace and grace to handle. We aren't going down if Jesus is on our boat amid the strongest storm we have ever seen. The winds may whip around us, the rain may pour down on us, and the thunder may crash as loud as it can, but we aren't going down.

I had one exceptionally rough day during my severe panic attacks. Actually, it was more like I had three good days; the rest were horrendous. On this particular day, I was tremoring non-stop and felt like my skin was crawling with anxiety and nerves that I just couldn't shake. It took everything in me to get through the workday.

While driving home, which was a grueling twenty-minute drive, I noticed dark storm clouds behind me. Watching the clouds, I started picturing them to be my anxiety and fears—the dark, stormy areas of my life from which I couldn't break free. Right on the other side of the line of dark clouds was a break, and clear skies were up ahead, just barely out of reach. As I surveyed the clouds, I said to myself, "The clear skies up ahead are where I break free from these dark storms of panic."

As I drove home, I kept this visual in my mind. Every few minutes scanning the sky to see if I had outrun the dark storm clouds yet, I would notice a car in front or beside me driving slowly, which in turn, slowed me down. I started thinking of these cars as "blocks" that satan puts in our way when trying to break free from the bondages he sets in our lives. As I switched lanes, I pictured myself avoiding each "block" meant to slow me down and hold me back from my goal of being free from all the anxiety and panic looming above and behind me in the dark clouds.

I switched lanes a few times and was finally about to break free so that the clear skies were above me when the road took a turn. The dark clouds came back over my car and stretched far ahead in front of me again. I was utterly discouraged but then reminded myself that just like the road, life takes turns. Sometimes you will have a breakthrough that will last for a short time. Then you will have a setback that causes you to fight in order to break free again, requiring you to strategically shift around "blocks" set up by the adversary and press on towards the clear skies ahead, where freedom awaits you.

At the end of my commute, I was at home under clear skies, but the dark clouds were approaching with a vengeance. It soon started to rain, and I realized two important truths: 1) Storms will come. No matter who you are, storms will come. If you aren't in one now, brace yourself because the Christian life is not free from storms. 2) Not all storms are in the forecast, so instead of focusing on the storm, we must focus on who is with us in the storm—Who is with us while we face the storms and most importantly, whom we choose to weather the storms of life with.

So, the next time you face a storm, remind yourself that it won't last forever. No matter what, Jesus is in your boat, and if He is in your boat, it can't sink, which means you, my dear brothers and sisters, won't sink either.

# CHAPTER 9: MEET ME IN THE MIDDLE

*"When you pass through the waters, I will be with you; and when you pass through the rivers, they will not sweep over you. When you walk through the fire, you will not be burned; the flames will not set you ablaze."* –Isaiah 43:2 (NIV)

Jesus promises us two important things in the Bible: 1) The world will give us trouble, and 2) He will be with us. Many times in life, you will be faced with a circumstance and unable to escape it, no matter how hard you try. No matter what route you take, there is generally only one way out, and that's by going through. Through is a scary concept that can paralyze anyone who fears the unknown.

People in general like to know how things will turn out, what the outcome will be in advance, and to be given an option. It is terrifying when faced with a struggle and only given the choice of going through or being destroyed by fear, panic, addiction and depression. You either remain in a depressed, anxious state or choose to move forward blindly, not knowing what the future holds. You take a chance on going through, because it HAS to be better than what you are currently experiencing.

Deuteronomy 31:8 (NIV) says, *"The Lord Himself goes before you and will be with you; He will never leave you nor forsake you. Do not be afraid; do not be discouraged."* Just because we do not see a way to the other side of our struggle doesn't mean that our loving Savior isn't already there, preparing a way. We try to handle so much on our own and forget that we have a God who is ALWAYS in control.

Control is hard to hand over and even more challenging when we haven't worked on building a solid relationship with Jesus. You wouldn't just hand over your house keys to a stranger and ask them to house-sit while you go on vacation, right? The same goes for your life.

Suppose you don't know Jesus as a best friend, a confidant, someone you can rely on with anything and everything that comes your way. In that case, you will have a really tough time going through and handing over your struggles to the Lord. I know this because going "through" and surrendering my panic, my depression, and my anxiety to Jesus was the most difficult challenge I have ever faced.

In life, we, unfortunately, become jaded by human interactions. People will let us down, leave us feeling empty, or worse, put us in positions where we're forced to be in control over things that aren't entirely our responsibility. We start to think that if we don't handle the situation, then no one will and something terrible will happen. These life experiences can beat you down and, over time, make you less willing to let anyone else have control. You get so used to handling everything on your own that you don't even know how to let someone help even if it's appropriate for them to share the burden with you.

Unfortunately, this includes Jesus. We lump Him in with everyone else because it's easier than opening ourselves up to being hurt again. I had experienced many different relationships where I felt I had to be in control. They left me feeling lost, lonely, and completely depleted of all energy; stuck in an unhealthy routine of survival mode. Unfortunately, when we are in or exposed to these relationships for too long, it becomes "normal" to us that we have to handle everything. This is a tool that satan uses to drive a wedge between us and the Lord. If he can get us to be in control at all times, it certainly makes it difficult for God to do His job.

I got to a point where I told myself that I "fully trusted" God; however, I kept incessantly checking my blood sugar with the monitor, which kept me still feeling like I had some control. One thing about God is that He wants complete obedience, not partial or half obedience. I was holding onto a thread of control while trying to give God the rest. Although I was seeing some positive results, I wasn't experiencing complete freedom from my panic, addiction and anxiety. The day I decided to give it ALL to God was when I allowed Him to take complete control and begin working His wonders in my life. Was it easy? Umm... NO!

It was definitely NOT easy, and I can't tell you how many times I started to completely surrender, got halfway through my day, and fell right back into my same old comfort zone of checking my sugar levels. This went on for almost a year. Did I feel defeated when this happened? YES. Every. Single. Time. But I knew that God was working with me, and eventually, one day, I would break free from my bondage.

I find it funny that we humans think we know better than God. Looking back, I think to myself, *Good grief! Did I seriously think that I could handle my panic attacks by myself better than God could?* Again, this is another lie that satan likes to tell us. He knows that God has the power to release us and bring us through anything we face, so we are told lies that we have to handle everything on our own, that we have the best solution, and that only we can solve our own problems. Many people in the Bible had to go through a challenging situation. Eventually, they had to decide to give the circumstance to the Lord and let Him do His work.

When we go through something difficult, it allows God to reveal Himself to us, changing us in the best way possible. Going through allows God to show His glory through our unimaginable situation.

Daniel Chapter 3 gives us the story of Shadrach, Meshach, and Abednego. These three men were friends of Daniel's and were appointed to oversee the affairs in the province of Babylon. King Nebuchadnezzar had a golden idol constructed and, in verse 6, declares, *"Whoever does not fall down, and worship shall that very hour be cast into the midst of a burning fiery furnace."* If you skip to verse 8, you see a group of Chaldean men show up and make accusations against Shadrach, Meshach, and Abednego. How many of us know that when we are trying to do the right thing, Satan ALWAYS puts someone or something in our path to cause a disturbance. These Chaldean men were there purely because they didn't like the Jews and saw the three as easy targets.

There will be many times when people come against you simply because they don't like you, and you have no idea why. At these times and in these moments, you need to not be bothered by their accusations and focus all of your energy and emotion on God and His approval.

Skip to verse 15; King Nebuchadnezzar is furious and has the three men brought before him for questioning. The three men, after being asked, *"Who is that god who can deliver you out of my hands?"* respond so firmly and confidently in verse 16-18: *"Oh Nebuchadnezzar, it is not necessary for us to answer you on this point. If our God whom we serve is able to deliver us from the burning fiery furnace, He will deliver us out of your hand, O King. But if not, let it be known to you, O King, that we will not serve your gods or worship the golden image which you have set up."* Shadrach, Meshach, and Abednego faced a dire and scary situation. I am pretty sure fear consumed them as they were called forth for questioning; however, they knew their God was greater. They didn't make excuses or try to cover up what they were doing for the Lord; they stood their ground. I love that they say, *if* their God was able to deliver them. They didn't know if it was in His plan, but they trusted their lives with Him anyway. Their courage and faith stayed strong in the presence of very real danger.

In verse 19 Nebuchadnezzar becomes enraged and now commands that the furnace be turned seven times hotter than usual. As if that wasn't enough, Verse 20 says that he also had the three men bound by the strongest men of the army. Verse 22 says that the fire was so hot that the men handling them were killed by the sparks and flames coming out of the furnace. So, now the three men were bound up and witnessing their handlers die as they prepared to enter the scorching furnace.

Have you ever felt like you were trying to get closer to God, and satan came in and started turning up the anxiety, the fears, the addiction and the depression to level seven? Then as if that's not good enough, you get tied up… not in a physical bondage but a mental bondage of hopelessness. Maybe it was your past coming back to haunt you. Perhaps it was one failure after another, and you started to doubt your worth. Perhaps you become so consumed with your inner thoughts that you feel frozen, unable to break free from the panic consuming you. Satan wants you to doubt what you are doing. He wants you to question your breakthrough, and he wants you to doubt God. Verse 23, *"And these three men, Shadrach, Meshach and Abednego fell down bound into the burning fiery furnace."*

This is the part of your life where you feel all hope is lost. You did everything you could do, and now you are entirely consumed, tied up, and engulfed in the very real fear right in front of you. With only your faith left as you fight to breathe, God shows up. (Verse 24), *"Then Nebuchadnezzar the King was astounded, and he jumped up and said to his counselors, 'Did we not cast three men bound into the midst of the fire?' They answered, 'True O King.'"* (Verse 25), *"He answered, 'Behold I see four men loose, walking in the midst of the fire, and they are not hurt! And the form of the fourth is like a son of the gods!'"* (Verse 26), *"Then Nebuchadnezzar came near to the mouth of the burning fiery furnace and said, 'Shadrach, Meshach and Abednego, you servants of the Most High God, come out and come here.' Then Shadrach, Meshach, and Abednego came out from the midst of the fire."* (Verse 27), *"And the Satraps, the deputies, the governors and the king's counselors gathered around together and saw these men-that the fire had no power upon their bodies, nor was the hair of their head singed; neither were their garments scorched or changed in color or condition, nor had even the smell of smoke clung to them."*

They had to go through the fiery furnace of fear, anxiety and a hopeless circumstance with certain death staring them in the face to show God's full glory and His goodness. I absolutely love that their reward wasn't just "surviving." It wasn't just barely making it through the terrible circumstance before them. God was faithful; He sent someone to comfort them and keep them safe as they went through the fiery furnace. God kept them perfectly intact as they went through; not even a hair on their heads or a piece of their clothing was singed or changed. Best of all, the witnesses to this miracle couldn't even smell smoke on Shadrach, Meshach, and Abednego as they emerged and stood outside the furnace. God not only brought them through but didn't leave any evidence of their terrifying experience lingering with them. They came out victorious on the other side of fear, hopelessness, and terror.

If you are going through something right now, and you don't see a way out, trust God. He is always faithful. Know that what you are going through is temporary. When you finally reach the other side, you will come out and not have any residue of the panic, hopelessness, and depression lingering on you anymore. Skip all the way to (verse 30), *"Then the king promoted Shadrach, Meshach and Abednego in the province of Babylon."* Not only did they make it through, but they were promoted!

God will never leave you stranded. He will take what the enemy worked so hard to destroy and use it for your good, to grow the kingdom and raise you to places you wouldn't have been able to on your own. Brothers and Sisters, we have a faithful God, so let's start placing our faith in Him; He never has and never will fail us.

Daniel Chapter 6 tells us the story of Daniel in the lion's den. King Darius gave Daniel the title of President over the 120 Satraps who ruled over the kingdom. There were two other presidents, but Verse 3 tells us, *"Then this Daniel was distinguished above the presidents and the satraps because an excellent spirit was in him."* When God allows us to be promoted to a position and distinguished because of our faith, we can almost always expect resistance from satan. (Verse 4) *"Then the presidents and satraps sought to find occasion (to bring accusation) against Daniel, concerning the kingdom, but they could find no occasion or fault, for he was faithful, nor was there any error or fault found in him."* We can sum this up with, "Haters gonna hate." There will always be haters against you when God has a blessing on your life.

Verse 7 says, *"All the presidents of the kingdom, the deputies and the satraps, the counselors and the governors, have consulted and agreed that the king should establish a royal statue and make a firm decree that whoever shall ask a petition of any god or man for thirty days, except of you, O King, shall be cast into the den of lions."* (Verse 8) *"Now O King, establish the decree and sign the writing that it may not be changed, according to the law of the Medes and the Persians, which cannot be altered."* (Verse 9) *"So King Darius signed the writing and the Decree."* Satan will stop at nothing to get to you; he will use anyone and anything to try and shake your foundation in Christ. Something important to note here is that King Darius was very fond of Daniel; he would never have wanted Daniel to be hurt; however, he was deceived by those around him, who had a hidden agenda, and blindly signed a decree without a second thought.

We need to ensure that we are always connected to the Holy Spirit, so if we are asked to do something, we don't just blindly do it; we ask for wisdom and guidance first. (Verse 10) *"Now when Daniel knew that the writing was signed, he went into his house, and his windows being open in his chamber toward Jerusalem, he got down upon his knees three times a day and prayed and gave thanks before his God, as he had done previously."* Daniel didn't care about the decree or the rules. He kept his focus on God and continued doing what he had always done, which was praying and giving thanks to God three times a day. So many times, in our life, we are put in predicaments where we feel like we need to "tone down" God to keep the relationship, the friendship, the job, etc. We have to choose between God and what the world wants. Daniel was wise enough to know that God's opinion was the only opinion that mattered, even if it meant death. (Verse 11), *"Then these men came thronging (by agreement) and found Daniel praying and making supplication (requests) before his God."* Then the men went to King Darius and essentially ratted Daniel out, demanding that King Darius stay true to his word and throw him into the den of lions. (Verse 14) *"Then the King, when he heard these words, was much distressed (over what he had done) and set his mind on Daniel to deliver him; and he labored until the sun went down to rescue him."* (Verse 15) *"Then these same men came thronging (by agreement) to the king and said, 'Know, O King, that it is a law of the Medes and Persians that no decree or statue which the king establishes may be changed or repealed.'"* Let's pause for a second and re-read the first part of verse 15, "Then the SAME men came to the king." When you are struggling with anxiety, panic, addiction and depression, it can feel like the same thoughts, negative mindset, and concerns come at you repeatedly, re-presenting your issues and never letting you forget that they are there.

It is important to remember what you have learned and speak back life and truth to the same thoughts that keep raging back. The thoughts you can't shake from your mind will try to keep you in bondage. Don't let them! Daniel had physical enemies coming at him, but as we continue, we can learn how to stand firm in our faith in God and come out victorious on the other side. (Verse 16) *"Then the king commanded, and Daniel was brought and cast into the den of lions. The king said to Daniel, 'May your God, whom you are serving continually, deliver you!'"* (Verse 17) *"And a stone was brought and laid upon the mouth of the den, and the king sealed it with his own signet and with the signet of his lords, that there might be no change of purpose concerning Daniel."* (Verse 18) *"Then the king went to his palace and passed the night fasting, neither were instruments of music or dancing girls brought before him; and his sleep fled from him."* (Verse 19) *"Then the king arose very early in the morning and went in haste to the den of lions."* (Verse 20) *"And when he came to the den and to Daniel, he cried out in a voice of anguish. The King said to Daniel, 'O Daniel, servant of the living God, is your God, Whom you serve continually, able to deliver you from the lions?'"*

Verses 16-20 are so profound. Now Daniel hasn't been delivered yet, there hasn't been a miracle yet. By all accounts, the ending doesn't look good for Daniel, yet King Darius, on the outside of Daniel's circumstance, had a little faith.

Let's pause here and go deeper. King Darius starts by referring to Daniel's God as the "Big G (not little g) God," meaning there was a sliver of belief and faith in King Darius toward Daniel's One true God. King Darius then tells Daniel, "May your God, Whom you are serving continually, deliver you!" King Darius references Daniel's devotion to continually serving his One true God. Then King Darius, after seeing Daniel sealed in the Lion's den, goes home and fasts. He fasts from earthly pleasures, and the Bible says he couldn't sleep all night. As soon as dawn breaks, King Darius goes in "haste" to the den of lions... another example of his mustard seed faith that Daniel's God could be the One true God. By all accounts, when someone is thrown into a lion's den, there should be no reason to check the following day to see if they are still alive…UNLESS…they believed that a miracle could happen, that Daniel's God, by some chance, would be able to deliver him and keep him safe.

Then, before Daniel even emerged from the Lion's den, King Darius showed one more small example of faith in Daniel's God. King Darius says to Daniel, *"O Daniel, servant of the living God, is your God, Whom you serve continually, able to deliver you from the Lions?"* King Darius speaks into what everyone else would consider, by all accounts, Daniel's grave, his death site, yet King Darius refers to Daniel's God as the "Living God."

You must always remember how crucial it is to surround yourself with God-fearing people. When we are stuck in the middle of what seems to be an unavoidable circumstance, (whether physically or in our minds), it is so important to have those outside of our circumstance speaking truth and believing in God for our deliverance. Daniel was trapped inside, just as many of you may feel trapped inside your body, struggling with addiction, or stuck in your mind as it swarms with panic and fear. Remember to keep close to your friends, relatives, co-workers, the church community, and all the people you can rely on to believe that the living God can see you through your circumstance and bring you THROUGH your struggle and into victory on the other side. (Verse 21) *"Then Daniel said to the king, 'O king, live forever!'"* (Verse 22) *"My God has sent His angel and has shut the lions' mouths so that they have not hurt me because I was found innocent and blameless before Him; and also, before you, O king (as you very well know) I have done no harm or wrong."* (Verse 23) *"Then the King was exceedingly glad and commanded that Daniel should be taken up out of the den. So, Daniel was taken up out of the den, and no hurt of any kind was found on him because he believed in his God."* (Verse 24) *"And the king commanded, and those men who had accused Daniel were brought and cast into the den of lions, they, their children and their wives; and before they ever reached the bottom of the den, the lions had overpowered them and had broken their bones in pieces."* (Verse 25) *"Then King Darius wrote to all peoples, nations, and languages (in his realm) that dwelt in all the earth: May peace be multiplied to you!"* (Verse 26) *"I make a decree that in all my royal dominion men must tremble and fear before the God of Daniel, for He is the Living God, enduring and steadfast forever, and His kingdom shall not be destroyed, and His dominion shall be even to the end (of the world)."* God sent an Angel to go THROUGH the lions' den with Daniel, the lions were taken care of, and Daniel came out without a scratch.

When God allows you to go through, He provides a way and a blessing on the other side. Without Daniel's devout and unwavering faith in the One true Living God, King Darius would never have had his faith strengthened, nor would he publicly declare Daniel's God the true God to all the people of the nations he governed.

Sometimes our struggle isn't about "us." It's about what God can do through us to make a difference in the world. Your struggle is your own; however, the victory after you have gone THROUGH belongs to the Lord.

Take a look at Moses. There is so much to say about Moses and his journey with God. In Exodus 3:19-20, God tells Moses from the burning bush, *"And I know that the King of Egypt will not let you go (unless forced to do so), no, not by a mighty hand. So, I will stretch out my hand and smite Egypt with all my wonders which I will do in it; and after that, he will let you go."* So, Moses started his journey with God, knowing that God would be with him, but also being warned that the journey would be difficult. One might consider Moses fortunate that God gave him the knowledge ahead of time that He would go through this with him; however, it's always easier to see how wonderful the works of God are when we look back and see the outcome from a finished standpoint.

Moses, in the middle of the journey, didn't know precisely how God would provide and therefore had to utilize his faith in God's promise to see him through. Moses's journey is unique because it shows God's unfailing love and understanding of our questioning human nature. Moses is concerned in Exodus Chapter 4, verse 1, and says, *"But behold, they will not believe me or listen to and obey my voice; for they will say 'The Lord has not appeared to you.'"* Pause right here. How many times do we hear from God, whether it's in our heart, our mind, or a special conviction/feeling that we know is coming from the Holy Spirit, and our first reaction is to think a negative thought against it and question what God is trying to tell us, or worse, try to talk ourselves out of it?

How comforting to know that Moses had a literal talking burning bush in front of him, and yet his first response was to question God and speak a negative thought, regarding God's direction. Thank goodness we have such a wonderful and patient God. (Verses 2-9) *"And the Lord said to him, 'What is that in your hand?' And he said 'A rod.' And He said, 'Cast it on the ground.' And he did so, and it became a serpent, and Moses fled from before it. And the Lord said to Moses, 'Put forth your hand and take it by the tail.' And he stretched out his hand and caught it, and it became a rod in his hand. (This you shall do, said the Lord), 'that the elders may believe that the Lord, the God of their fathers, of Abraham, of Isaac, and of Jacob, has indeed appeared to you.' The Lord said also to him, 'Put your hand into your bosom.' He put his hand into his bosom, and when he took it out, behold, his hand was leprous, as white as snow. (God) said, 'Put your hand into your bosom again.' So, he put his hand back into his bosom, and when he took it out, behold, it was restored as the rest of his flesh. (Then God said) 'If they will not believe you or heed the voice or the testimony of the first sign, they may believe the voice or the witness of the second sign. But if they will also not believe these two signs or heed your voice, you shall take some water out of the river (Nile) and pour it upon the dry Land; and the water which you take out of the river (Nile) shall become blood on the dry Land.'"*

I love that Moses had genuine fears and concerns that he brought forth to God, and God not only gave him one solution but rather three different solutions to ease Moses's fears. We have the God El Shaddai, The God of More than Enough. He has more than one solution for our problems, enough provision for us, and enough patience to walk us through the journey before us.

Now Verse 10 is where I really start to relate to Moses: *"And Moses said to the Lord, 'O Lord, I am not eloquent or a man of words, neither before nor since You have spoken to Your servant; for I am slow of speech and have a heavy and awkward tongue.'"* Moses jumps right from one concern to the next as he hears God's plan for his life. First, he is concerned no one will believe him when he says he spoke to the Lord. Now he's afraid he won't be able to accomplish what God wants because of his speech impediment and lack of verbal eloquence.

How many times do we do the same thing? God puts something on our hearts, and we come up with one reason after another as to why it isn't a good idea, why it won't work, why it's the wrong time, why the finances aren't there to sustain what God wants us to do, why it's too inconvenient. The list of excuses we tell ourselves goes on and on. I genuinely believe satan has a field day when it comes to God's direction and our internal response. Our hearts may want to do what God says, yet our minds will hesitate, waver, and reconsider the initial prompting we felt from the Holy Spirit.

When God's word promises over and over that we will be delivered from our fears, we need to take all of the negative thoughts and set them aside and focus on the truth of God's word. Good thing we are in good company with Moses! (Verse 11) *"And the Lord said to him, 'Who has made man's mouth? Or who makes the dumb, or the deaf, or the seeing, or the blind? Is it not I, the Lord?* (Verse 12) *Now therefore go, and I will be with your mouth and will teach you what you shall say.'"* After hearing that the Lord will now guide his words, Moses, in Verse 13, says, *"Oh, my Lord, I pray You, send by the hand of (some other) whom you will (send)."* The Lord promises to be with Moses, to guide his words and teach him what to say, and Moses, a third time, comes back at the Lord and begs for Him to choose someone else.

Brothers and sisters, how often are we given a struggle, a challenge, a panicked situation where there seems to be no way out? We beg and plead with God to "bless" someone else with this trial. Sometimes that may sound like, "God, please, I can't do this anymore. I know you are walking me through this struggle so that I can, in turn, help others, but I am just not strong enough. I don't have what it takes; there are others who are more qualified. I am tired and can't do what you are asking me to do."

Doing the will of God is not an easy task. We are called to look beyond our current circumstances and see the outcome as how it should be, not as it is currently, whether in conquering your panic attacks, your depression, your addiction, your loneliness, your weight loss journey that has taken over a decade, the strained relationships in your life, overcoming not just one, but multiple divorces, all of which left you feeling like you are less than worthy of God to use you for anything significant.

Moses teaches us here that God chooses not based on looks, appearance, intellect, strength, or how wonderful our vocabulary is. God chooses each one of us precisely because of the weaknesses we have. If God had picked a great orator to do Moses's job, don't you think the story would have turned out differently? A great orator could have convinced a crowd of anything. They would have been able to articulate their words so that they seemed to always be in control and have it all together. No, God chose Moses precisely because he had a speech impediment. He chose Moses for his weakness because the power of God could genuinely shine through his weakness. It is more impressive that a man with a speech impediment freed God's chosen people from the Egyptians. (NIV, 1 Corinthians 1:27), *"But God chose the foolish things in the world to shame the wise; God chose the weak things of the world to shame the strong."*

So, take a look at your life. Look where you may feel weak and unworthy. Then, open your heart to the Savior, asking Him to use you in every way possible; to allow His goodness and glory to shine through the less desirable parts of your life. (Verses 14-17) *"Then the anger of the Lord blazed against Moses; He said, 'Is there not Aaron your brother, the Levite? I know he can speak well. Also, he is coming out to meet you, and when he sees you, he will be overjoyed. You must speak to him and put the words in his mouth, and I will be with your mouth and with his mouth and will teach you what you shall do. He shall speak for you to the people, acting as a mouthpiece for you, and you shall be as God to him. And you shall take the rod in your hand with which you shall work the signs (that prove I sent you).'"* God understood the human nature of Moses, and He understood his concerns, yet God refused to use anyone besides Moses. God even mentions that Aaron is a great speaker but doesn't give up on Moses and move on to Aaron. God allows Aaron to be another tool for Moses to utilize in completing the task set before him. It's no wonder Aaron was Moses' brother; God knows all and had already prepared help for Moses, giving Aaron a talent years before Moses knew he needed it. Now that's an extraordinary God!

No matter what we face and what we are going through, God has already prepared the right people to come into our lives at the right time to help us navigate our fears. Moses and Aaron began their journey to Egypt, and if we go to the last verses of Exodus Chapter 4, Verses 29-31, *"Moses and Aaron went and gathered together (In Egypt) all the elders of the Israelites. Aaron spoke all the words which the Lord had spoken to Moses and did the signs in the sight of the people. And the people believed; and when they heard that the Lord had visited the Israelites, and that He had looked (in compassion) upon their affliction, they bowed their heads and worshipped."* How wonderful for Moses that his first concern was taken care of by the Lord. The people believed he was indeed sent to free them from the bondage they had been experiencing. With this encouragement, Exodus Chapter 5 begins Moses and Aaron's journey of confidently asking Pharaoh to "Let my people go." Throughout the next five chapters, Moses and Aaron will ask Pharaoh to "Let my people go" eight times.

How often do you find yourself saying, "Let my anxiety go! Let my depression go! Let my addiction go! Let my panic and overwhelming sense of dread GO!" How frustrating when we demand, we fight, we beg and plead for our problem to leave so we can live the life Christ died for us to live, yet the answer is "NO."

In Exodus Chapter 5, we see the first account of this struggle between freedom and captivity. (Verse 1-2) *"Afterward, Moses and Aaron went in and told Pharaoh, 'Thus says the Lord, the God of Israel, let my people go, that they may hold a feast to Me in the wilderness.' But Pharaoh said, 'Who is the Lord, that I should obey His voice to let Israel go? I know not the Lord, neither will I let Israel go.'"* Jumping to Verses 6-9, we see the tightening of the bondage on the Israelites, *"The very same day Pharaoh commanded the taskmasters of the people and their officers, 'You shall no more give the people straw to make brick; let them go and gather straw for themselves. But the number of the bricks which they made before you shall still require of them; you shall not diminish it in the least. For they are idle; that is why they cry, 'Let us go and sacrifice to our God.' Let heavier work be laid upon the men that they may labor at it and pay no attention to lying words.'"*

Let's pause here and insert the devil into Pharaoh's position. When we worship God and feel as though He has heard our cry to help us in our time of desperation, we are just like the Israelites in Egypt who finally feel remembered by God and bow down and worship Him. We get angry at the adversary and say, "Leave me alone! Let me go! Stop troubling me!" Although God has the ultimate power to step in at any moment and relieve us from our struggle, most of the time, He doesn't because you can't have growth without struggle. So, God will sometimes allow the enemy to test and try us until we are spiritually ready to move forward in God's plan for our life.

This results in satan attacking us mentally even harder than before. We feel overwhelmed, emotions pile up, feelings bring us down, depression worsens, and the nagging negative thoughts become unbearable as we try to still complete our day-to-day tasks. One could say that satan, just like Pharaoh, distracts us with heavy bondage, so we don't have time to listen to the word of God, or in Pharaoh's case, the "Lying words of Moses."

Satan's goal is to keep us locked in the life we have so we can't move forward into the life God has for us, just like Pharaoh wanted to keep the Israelites locked in Egypt, far away from their longed-for Promised Land.

Now let's jump to Verses 20-23, *"And the foremen met Moses and Aaron, who were standing in the way as they came forth from Pharaoh. And the foremen said to them, 'The Lord look upon you and judge, because you have made us a rotten stench to be detested by Pharaoh and his servants and have put a sword in their hand to slay us.' Then Moses turned again to the Lord and said, 'O Lord, why have you dealt evil to this people? Why did you ever send me? For since I came to Pharaoh to speak in Your name, he has done evil to this people, neither have You delivered Your people at all.'"*

So, at this point, Moses is starting to feel the intensity of the issue at hand. I love that Moses goes right to the Lord and questions Him. Haven't we all felt that way at least once in our lives? You try to do the right thing, and then suddenly you get dealt a crappy hand, and you're like, "Come on, God. I sacrificed all of this for You, and my situation is going to get worse?! What gives?" Moses went from being the deliverer sent by God to probably the most despised man amongst the Israelites, in only a few hours. How scary when you don't know God's plan and have to rely on faith to take you through to the next step of your journey.

Chapter 6, Verses 1-2 say, *"Then the Lord said to Moses, 'Now you shall see what I will do to Pharaoh; for by a strong hand he will (not only) let them go, but he will drive them out of his Land with a strong hand.' And God said to Moses, 'I am the Lord.'"* In Verses 3-8, the Lord reminds Moses of who He is, what His covenant was with the Israelites, and that He heard and remembered their cries. Moses goes back to the Israelites and tells them all the Lord revealed to him, and they refuse to listen to Moses because of their anguish and cruel bondage.

Relatable? Yes! When life kicks you down, it takes a LOT to get back up, keep going, and keep believing and trusting that it will get better. (Verse 12) *"But Moses said to the Lord, Behold (my own people) the Israelites have not listened to me; how then shall Pharaoh give heed to me, who am of deficient and impeded speech?"*

I LOVE this. So far, nothing has been going as planned for Moses. He is discouraged and feels like God's plan will never come true. Moses goes to the Lord in prayer and not only expresses his frustrations, but he goes right back to his initial fear, the fear that because he is slow in speech, he won't be able to carry out the plan God has set before him. Don't we all do this? When we pray for God to guide us and deliver us from the anxiety, depression, addiction, and fear that is very present in our day-to-day lives, we can feel abandoned, hopeless and often revert to focusing on the bondages that have held us back instead of the truths God has promised and spoken.

The Lord then reminds Moses and Aaron that they will bring the Israelites out of the Land of Egypt. The Lord reminds them of their genealogy and why they were chosen for a specific purpose. Then the Lord commands Moses to tell Pharaoh all He has told him. (Verse 30) *"But Moses said to the Lord, 'Behold, I am of deficient and impeded speech; how then shall Pharaoh listen to me?'"*

Oh, Moses…how I relate to you. Sometimes the Lord can speak every truth to your heart, yet your mind focuses only on fear, negative thoughts, and concerns, negating all God promised for your life. This is Moses's third time bringing up his "disability and biggest fear" to the Lord. How often do we focus on what's wrong with us instead of listening to everything God says is right about us? (Chapter 7 Verses 1-6) *"The LORD said to Moses, 'Behold, I make you as God to Pharaoh; and Aaron your brother shall be your prophet. You shall speak all that I commanded you, and Aaron your brother shall tell Pharaoh to let the Israelites go out of his Land. And I will make Pharaoh's heart stubborn and hard, and multiply My signs, My wonders, and miracles in the land of Egypt. But Pharaoh will not listen to you, and I will lay My hand upon Egypt and bring forth My hosts. My people the Israelites, out of the land of Egypt by great acts of judgment. The Egyptians shall know that I am the Lord when I stretch forth my hand upon Egypt and bring out the Israelites from among them.' And Moses and Aaron did so, as the Lord commanded them."* On eight separate occasions, between Chapters 7 and 12, Moses and Aaron made their request to Pharaoh. Each time saying,

"Let my people go!" and each time being told, "No." They were then told by God to preform various miracles/plagues to convince Pharaoh to do as they asked.

I used to think, "If God can do anything instantly, why did Moses and Aaron have to do this back and forth 8 times?" I genuinely believe that it was needed not because God needed it to deliver the Israelites but because Moses and Aaron needed it to strengthen their faith and confidence in the word of God. Over these chapters, the word continually states, *"And the Lord hardened Pharaoh's stubborn heart, and he did not let the Israelites out of his land."*

Sometimes the Lord will harden the situation we are facing in order to put us in a position where we have to rely on Him. As we face each challenge and obstacle, we slowly grow our faith and confidence in the Lord, and, little by little, we get closer and closer to our deliverance. Every time Pharaoh said, "No," Moses and Aaron had to draw deeper in their faith and stand firm, knowing that God was stronger than the adversary before them.

When we are faced with an unbearable situation, panic attacks, fear, anxiety, depression the bondage of addiction, we must remember to stand firm in faith just like Moses and Aaron did, allowing God to work His wonders in our life so that we can also be freed from everything satan is using to hold us back.

As you may well know, the last plague left all of the first-born Egyptians, including Pharaoh's son, dead. Chapter 12 vs 31, *"He (Pharaoh) called for Moses and Aaron by night and said, 'Rise up, get out from among my people, both you and the Israelites; and go, serve the Lord as you said.'"* (Verse 40-41) *"Now the time the Israelites dwelt in Egypt was 430 years. At the end of the 430 years, even that very day, all the hosts of the Lord went out of Egypt."* 430 years is a LONG time to wait for deliverance.

Everyone can relate to waiting on the Lord, and sometimes the wait seems so long you feel forgotten by God. This passage is a wonderful reminder that God's timing is always perfect. God heard the Israelites' cry, yet He waited on the right timing for their deliverance. God has precisely the right time for your deliverance too! It may not be when you want it, but it will be when you need it the most. Believe with everything you are that when God chooses to move, nothing can stop Him. Just like Moses and Aaron stood firm in their belief that God would eventually deliver the Israelites out of Pharaoh's hands, we, too, must stand firm in our beliefs. Chapter 13, Verses 21-22, "*The Lord went before them by day in a pillar of cloud to lead them along the way and by night in a pillar of fire to give them light, that they might travel by day and by night. The pillar of cloud by day and fire by night did not depart from before the people."*

When God leads you out of a situation, He stays with you. Just like the Israelites had the pillar of fire and cloud to lead them, we are given the Holy Spirit to reside in us and guide us continually through our journey. Chapter 14, Verses 8-10, *"The Lord made hard and strong the heart of Pharaoh king of Egypt, and he pursued the Israelites, for (they) left proudly and defiantly. The Egyptians pursued them, all the horses and chariots of Pharaoh and his horsemen and his army and overtook them encamped at the (Red) Sea by Pi-hahiroth, in from of Baal-zephon. When Pharaoh drew near, the Israelites looked up, and behold, the Egyptians were marching after them; and the Israelites were exceedingly frightened and cried out to the Lord."* (Verse 13) *"Moses told the people, 'Fear not; stand still (firm, confident, undismayed) and see the salvation of the Lord which He will work for you today! For the Egyptians you have seen today you shall never see again.* (Verse 14) *The Lord will fight for you, and you shall hold your peace and remain at rest.'"* (Verse 15) *"The Lord said to Moses, 'Why do you cry to me? Tell the people of Israel to go forward!'"* (Verse 16) *"Lift up your rod and stretch out your hand over the sea and divide it, and the Israelites shall go on dry ground through the midst of the sea."* (Verse 17) *"And I, behold, I will harden (make stubborn and strong) the hearts of the Egyptians, and they shall go (into the sea) after them; and I will gain honor over Pharaoh, and all his host, his chariots and horsemen."* (Verse 20) *"Coming between the host of Egypt and the host of Israel. It was a cloud and darkness to the Egyptians, but it gave light by night to the Israelites; and the one host did not come by the other all night."* (Verse 21) *Then Moses stretched out his hand over the sea, and the Lord caused the sea to go back by a strong east wind all that night and made the sea dry land; and the waters were divided.* (Verse 22) *And the Israelites went into the midst of the sea on dry ground, the waters being a wall to them on their right hand and on their left."* (Verse 23) *"The Egyptians pursued and went in after them into the midst of the sea, even all Pharaoh's horses, his chariots and his horsemen."* (Verse 24) *"And in the morning watch the Lord through the pillar of fire and cloud looked down on the host of the Egyptians and discomfited (them)."*

I absolutely LOVE seeing the progression of Moses's relationship with the Lord. At the beginning of his journey, he was afraid. He questioned his ability to carry out the plan God set before him. Fast forward-we are now at the Red Sea, the Egyptians are coming up close behind the Israelites, everyone is freaking out, and Moses is calm, cool, and collected. His response in this situation differs significantly from his initial responses to God's direction.

This time, instead of seeing a scary obstacle in front of him, he, without even thinking, says in response to the people's cries., *"Fear not! Stand still and see the salvation of the Lord, which He will work for you today!"* Moses had built such a relationship with the Lord that he knew without a shadow of a doubt that if the Lord said He would deliver them, there was no reason to panic.

It's wonderful that God strengthened Moses' faith before presenting him with such a stressful situation. Many times in our journey, we feel like we are confronted with one circumstance after another, causing us to consciously decide to dig deeper into our faith and stand firm in the word of God. I love God's response to Moses after hearing the people's cries: *"The Lord said to Moses, 'Why do you cry to me? Tell the people of Israel to go forward!'"* (Verse 16) *"Lift up your rod and stretch out your hand over the sea and divide it, and the Israelites shall go on dry ground through the midst of the sea.'"*

Through…the Lord needed them to stop panicking, press on *through* the feelings of fear and anxiety, and go into the unknown, where He would lead them to freedom on the other side. God made a way when there seemed to be no way. He held true to His promises and never left them stranded in panic. Just like He kept His promise to Moses and the Israelites, He will also keep His promise to see you through your struggles. Remember Jesus's Promise #1: the world will give us trouble and Promise #2: He will always be with us.

Brothers and sisters, no matter what circumstance, what fear, what anxiety, what unbearable situation is staring you in the face, you have Jehovah Shammah, the God who is ALWAYS there, walking with you every step of the way. Take a breath, stand your ground, and declare with all your might, "Today is the day! I am going THROUGH with the one and only God Who can and will see me through. The one and only God, Who can keep me safe when I'm walking through the fires of anxiety that consume me.

To the one and only God, Who can keep me safe and walk me through the attacks of others who are out to get me.

To the one and only God, Who keeps me safe and walks me through when I am thrown into the midst of adversity for doing what's right. When I am surrounded by the roaring Lion who is seeking to devour me at any second, I remind myself that I have the Living God who will go through the attack with me and can shut the mouth of that Lion and keep me safe.

I praise God that when I hit the roadblock of the giant sea that is raging against me while the enemy is chasing me down, coming up quickly behind me, I know that I have El Shaddai, the God Who is more than enough. The God Who can part the waters in front of me and lead me through to the other side of safety when all viable options of escape are gone.

There is only one way to get to the other side of your fear, anxiety, panic, addiction, and depression, and that is by going through with the only One Who promises to meet you in the middle of your mess and see you through to victory on the other side.

# CHAPTER 10: FORGOTTEN

*"After all, God is God because He remembers."* –Elie Wiesel

What do you do when you feel like God has forgotten you? In the previous chapter, we read about God delivering many different people from extremely dangerous, scary, and uncertain circumstances, but what do you do when you feel like God has forgotten you altogether? Sometimes in the middle of our struggles, we feel like God is nowhere to be found—that our situation is hopeless and of no concern to the One Who created the Heavens and the Earth. It may even seem like He has time to worry about everyone else besides you.

You could be watching everyone around you find happiness in marriage. At the same time, you are desperately praying that God sends you the right spouse as relationship after relationship fail. You could have waited through infertility appointment after infertility appointment with no luck, going home constantly discouraged. At the same time, your friends are welcoming babies into their homes. You could have been struggling with addiction, panic, anxiety, and depression. You wonder why, when you look around, it seems like you are the only one experiencing these struggles and others seem to not have a care in the world.

Feeling forgotten is a hopeless and discouraging feeling. Satan thrives on isolating us from God and His goodness. In the in-between moments, where we feel like we are all alone and our desperate prayers have fallen on deaf ears, we must remind ourselves that despite how the circumstance may look, God is still very present and with us every step of the way.

One of my favorite poems is "Footprints in the Sand." I treasure this poem and would read it whenever I felt alone or abandoned by God.

**Footprints in the Sand**
"One night, I dreamed a dream.
As I was walking along the beach with my Lord.
Across the dark sky flashed scenes from my life.
For each scene, I noticed two sets of footprints in the sand,
One belonging to me and one to my Lord.
After the last scene of my life flashed before me,
I looked back at the footprints in the sand.
I noticed that at many times along the path of my life,
especially at the very lowest and saddest times,
there was only one set of footprints.
This really troubled me, so I asked the Lord about it.
'Lord, You said once I decided to follow You,
You'd walk with me all the way.
But I noticed that during the saddest and most troublesome times of my life, there was only one set of footprints. I don't understand why, when I needed You the most, You would leave me.'
He whispered, 'My precious child, I love you and will never leave you. Never, ever, during your trials and testings. When you saw only one set of footprints, It was then that I carried you'."

How comforting to know that even when we can't feel or see God, He always shows up when we need Him most. Many people in the Bible have felt completely forgotten and abandoned by God. Abraham (Abram) and Sarah (Sarai) in the Old Testament were told to leave their country, relatives, and friends and travel to a land the Lord would show them. The promise given to Abraham in Genesis Chapter 12:2-3 (NIV) is: *"I will make you into a great nation, and I will bless you; I will make your name great, and you will be a blessing. I will bless those who bless you, and whoever curses you I will curse; and all peoples on earth will be blessed through you."* What an incredible blessing!

So, at seventy-five, Abram (Abraham), his wife Sarai (Sarah), and his nephew Lot left *everything* behind to go to Canaan to fulfill the promises of the Lord. The journey was long, and they faced many challenges along the way. In Genesis Chapter 15, verses 1-6, *"After these things, the word of the Lord came to Abram in a vision, saying, 'Fear not, Abram, I am your Shield, your abundant compensation and your reward shall be exceedingly great.' And Abram said, 'Lord God, what can You give me, since I am going on childless, and he who shall be the owner and heir of my house is this Eliezer of Damascus?' And Abram continued, 'Look, You have given me no child; and (a servant) born in my house is my heir.' And behold, the word of the Lord came to him, saying, 'This man shall not be your heir, but he who shall come from your own body shall be your heir.' And He brought him outside (his tent into the starlight) and said, 'Look now toward the heavens and count the stars if you are able to number them.' Then He said to him, 'So shall your descendants be.' And he (Abram) believed in the Lord, and he counted it to him as righteousness (right standing with God)."*

So now Abram has just received yet another extraordinary promise from God, this time that he will have an heir, and his descendants will outnumber the stars. How wonderful for Abram to directly hear from God and be given such an incredible promise! Wouldn't it be wonderful if we heard a promise from God and then got a fairly quick response to the promise spoken in our hearts?

Unfortunately for Abram, the fulfillment of his promise was about twenty-four years away. In Chapter 16, just one chapter after the incredible promise from God, Sarai had still not produced any children for Abram, so she took matters into her own hands and gave Abraham Hagar, her Egyptian maidservant, to take and have children with. (Verse 2) *"And Sarai said to Abram, 'See here, the Lord has restrained me from bearing (children). I am asking you to have intercourse with my maid; it may be that I can obtain children by her.' And Abram listened to and heeded what Sarai said."*

Sarai and Abram were both impatient. As we know, being impatient leads to us trying to take control of the situation instead of letting God work in His own timing. It took about four verses for Sarai to figure out that this was a bad idea. As soon as Hagar became pregnant, she quickly regretted her actions.

How many of us wait on the Lord, and when the timing isn't what we were expecting or wanted, we take matters into our own hands? We justify, "Well, God should have had this answered/taken care of by now," or "Maybe I didn't hear God clearly enough." When we decide to take matters into our own hands and rush God's timing, the results are rarely good. We tend to add obstacles and trials that keep us in the 'wilderness' of our situation longer than if we had just waited on the Lord.

The Bible says that Abram was 86 when Ishmael, the son of Hagar was born. So, Abram's promises first began at the age of seventy-five. Eleven years later, he had a son by Sarai's maidservant. In Chapter 17 Abram is now ninety-nine years old and hears from God again with yet another promise. I love that even though Abram and Sarai muddied the waters of God's plan, God still showed up and continued His promises.

There have been so many times in my life when I thought I had let God down and ruined His plans for me. It is wonderful to know that even when we have entirely failed by all human accounts, God is there to pick up the pieces, take our mess and weave it into the most beautiful message.

Throughout chapter 17, God promises Abram again in verse 2, *"And I will make My covenant between Me and you and will multiply you exceedingly."* Twenty-four years later and God is still speaking life into Abram's seemingly dead situation. God then changes Abram's name to Abraham, which means, "father of many." Jumping to Verse 6, God promises to make kings come from his bloodline (which foreshadows Jesus' birth). (Verse 7), *"And I will establish My covenant between Me and you and your descendants after you throughout their generations for an everlasting, solemn pledge, to be a God to you and to your posterity (all future generations) after you."* God then gives Abraham a covenantal promise, stating that all males must be circumcised (how popular Abraham must have been!).

Then we jump to Verse 15: *"And God said to Abraham, 'As for Sarai your wife, you shall not call her name Sarai; but Sarah (Princess) her name shall be.'"* (Verse 16), *"And I will bless her and give you a son also by her. Yes, I will bless her, and she shall be a mother of nations; kings of peoples shall come from her."* (Verse 17) *"Then Abraham fell on his face and laughed and said in his heart, 'Shall a child be born to a man who is a hundred years old? And shall Sarah, who is ninety years old, bear a son?'"* (Verse 18) *"And (he) said to God, 'Oh that Ishmael might live before you!'"* (Verse 19) *"But God said, 'Sarah your wife shall bear you a son indeed, and you shall call his name Isaac (laughter); and I will establish My covenant or my solemn pledge with him for an everlasting covenant and with his posterity after him."'* (Verse 20) *"And as for Ishmael, I have heard and heeded you; Behold, I will bless him and will make him fruitful and will multiply him exceedingly; He will be the Father of twelve princes, and I will make him a great nation."* (Verse 21) *"But My covenant, my promise and pledge, I will establish with Isaac, whom Sarah will bear to you at this season next year."* (Verse 22) *"And God stopped talking with him and went up from Abraham."*

God promised Abram, but first, he needed to mold Abram into Abraham. Sometimes God puts a promise on our hearts. The time between the promise and the deliverance is where God molds us, where He tests our perseverance, our faith, our steadfastness, and where He shapes us into everything we need to be by cutting away everything we have clung onto from the world.

When God was ready to fulfill Abram's promise, He first gave him a new identity. Brothers and sisters, your old identity as depressed, addicted, anxious, and panicked is in your past! You have a new name as a child of God. Beautiful things will happen in your life, but, like Abraham and Sarah, you must believe, be steadfast, and, most of all, trust that God's plan is better than any plan you had for yourself.

So, no matter if it takes twenty-four hours or twenty-four years to reach a point when you feel most forgotten by God, you must remind yourself that His promises will prevail, and you will see His glory in your life at just the right time. In Chapter 18 there is still no baby; the Lord visits Abraham and in Verse 10 says, *"I will surely return to you when the season comes round, and behold, Sarah your wife will have a son." And Sarah was listening and heard it at the tent door which was behind Him."* (Verse 11) *"Now Abraham and Sarah were old, well advanced in years; it had ceased to be with Sarah as with (young) women." (She was past the age of childbearing).* (Verse 12) *"Therefore Sarah laughed to herself, saying, 'After I have become aged shall I have pleasure and delight, my lord (husband) also being old?'"* (Verse13) *"And the Lord asked Abraham, 'Why did Sarah laugh, saying, Shall I really bear a child when I am so old?'"* (Verse 14) *"Is anything too hard or wonderful for the Lord? At the appointed time, when the season (for her delivery) comes around, I will return to you and Sarah shall have borne a son."* Jump all the way to Chapter 21, Verse 1, *"The Lord visited Sarah as He had said, and the Lord did for her as He had promised."* Read that one more time. The Lord did for her *as He had promised.* Brothers and sisters, the Lord has promises for your life. Promises that have been written on your heart and spoken over you since birth. When the time is right, the Lord will put all the broken pieces of your life back together. I relate so much to the humanity of Abraham and Sarah. How forgotten they must have felt waiting and waiting for the Lord's promises to come true. I can only imagine how hopeless they felt as Sarah approached and surpassed her childbearing years. They must have been so frustrated constantly hearing God's promise and then looking around at what appeared to be no progress in their situation. At some point, they must have felt crazy and questioned whether God really did promise them a child.

As the years went on with promise after promise and every possible earthly solution slowly slipping away, the constant undertone of their life remained forgotten. I love that in Verse 12, Sarah laughs at the Lord's promise. When she was younger, sure, the promise was great. Now she is old, and I can only imagine her thinking, "Really, God? Now? I'm old. You wait for me to be fragile, old, and tried to now muster up the strength to carry, deliver, and raise a child?"

How often do we try to plan our lives out and then get thrown a curve ball that messes up our "perfect" plan? Sarah must have been prepared for years to have her son. Now that she is old, she has to adjust her plans and prepare to have a son in a completely different set of circumstances. God's response in verse 14 is everything we need to hear, *"Is there anything too hard or wonderful for the Lord? At the appointed time, when the season (for her delivery) comes around, I will return to you, and Sarah shall have borne a son."*

When panicked, depressed, and anxious, remind yourself that there is NOTHING too hard for the Lord. Feeling forgotten amid complete panic is lonely; it's sometimes depressing and downright terrifying. We must remember that during these times, we are not forgotten; we are in a waiting period. God is perfecting us and preparing us for our deliverance from every gripping fear.

At the appointed time, when the season for your deliverance from every bondage that is holding you back arrives, the Lord will show up, He will make His presence known, and you will give birth to all of the beautiful things that He has instilled, perfected and prepared inside of you. The light will break through the darkness that has consumed you, and the wholeness of life promised by our Lord will dwell within you. Verse 5, *"Abraham was a hundred years old when Isaac was born."* This was not in Abraham and Sarah's time but God's perfect time. Twenty-four years later, when the time was right for the Lord, He gave Abraham and Sarah the desires of their heart in the most miraculous way imaginable.

Hannah felt forgotten by God. In 1 Samuel Chapter 1, we read the story of Hannah and Peninnah, two women who were wives to Elkanah. Peninnah had borne multiple children; however, Hannah did not have any. Elkanah loved Hannah, and in Chapter 1, verse 5 it says, *"But to Hannah he gave a double portion, for he loved Hannah, but the Lord had given her no children."*

Hannah wanted nothing more than to be a mother. She was provoked by Peninnah, who reveled in the fact that she was given multiple children to raise. (Verse 7), *"So it was year after year; whenever Hannah went up to the Lord's house, Peninnah provoked her, so she wept and did not eat."*

Have you ever been in a situation where you were alone, struggling with your inner doubts, fears, and anxieties, and someone who seemed to have everything you wanted came along? They can go to the grocery store when it's a complete struggle for you to get out of your car and walk in. They can fall asleep peacefully while you are left with your mind racing with negative and terrifying thoughts that keep you up all night. They seem to enjoy every aspect of life without a care in the world, while you are anxious about the next basic task you must complete.

When these situations arise, it is so easy to feel forgotten. We start to question what we did wrong. Was God mad at us, and why did God find such favor with them and leave us alone at the bottom of the barrel? <u>Every day</u>, Hannah was reminded how she felt forgotten and how Peninnah seemed to have all of God's favor.

While they were in Shiloh worshipping the Lord, verse 10 says, *"And (Hannah) was in distress of soul, praying to the Lord and weeping bitterly.* (Verse 11) *She vowed, saying, 'O Lord of hosts, if You will indeed look on the affliction of Your handmaid and remember, and not forget Your handmaid but will give me a son, I will give him to the Lord all his life; no razor shall touch his head.'* (Verse 12) *And as she continued praying before the Lord, Eli noticed her mouth.* (Verse 13) *Hannah was speaking in her heart; only her lips moved but her voice was not heard. So, Eli (the Priest) thought she was drunk.* (Verse 14) *Eli said to her, 'How long will you be intoxicated? Put wine away from you.'* (Verse 15) *But Hannah answered, 'No my Lord, I am a woman of a sorrowful spirit. I have drunk neither wine nor strong drink, but I was pouring out my soul before the Lord.* (Verse 16) *Regard not your handmaid as a wicked woman; for out of my great complaint and bitter provocation I have been speaking.'"*

Hannah was distressed and weeping bitterly. How many of you have been so upset with the circumstance of your anxiety, addiction, depression, and panic that all you could do was cry the deepest cry you have ever cried, poured your heart out to the Lord, and felt the most immense distress in your soul? I've been there quite a few times. It is the most vulnerable state when you resort to begging and pleading with God, asking Him to simply remember you. (Verse 19) *"The family rose early the next morning, worshipped before the Lord, and returned to their home in Ramah. Elkanah knew Hannah, his wife, and the Lord remembered her.* (Verse 20) *Hannah became pregnant and, in due time, bore a son and named him Samuel (heard of God). Because she said, 'I have asked him of the Lord.'"*

At Hannah's deepest, saddest moment, the Lord remembered her. Brothers and sisters, at your deepest, saddest, loneliest moment, when you feel as though everyone around you is being blessed while you barely survive, rest assured that we have El Roi, the God Who sees and the God Who remembers. Hannah, in the pit of her agony, stayed faithful to God. What was on Hannah's heart was on God's mind. We have an incredibly faithful God Who will forever see our hurts and pain, and whatever we feel, He feels. You are not alone; you are remembered, you are loved, and you will be restored to all of the glory God has for you.

He was a shepherd boy long before David was King David the "Goliath slayer". Lost in the shuffle of seven older brothers, he spent most of his time alone, herding the flocks of sheep and talking to God.

In 1 Samuel Chapter 16, Samuel, the first Prophet after Moses, was sent by God to anoint the next King of Israel. Samuel arrived at the house of Jesse and, one by one, declined all seven of David's older brothers. Samuel, perplexed, says to Jesse in verse 11, *"Then he (Samuel) said to Jesse, 'Are all your sons here?' (Jesse) said, 'There is yet the youngest; he is tending the sheep.' Samuel said to Jesse, 'Send for him; for we will not sit down to eat until he is here.'"*

The word goes on to say that when David stood before Samuel, the Lord spoke and said at the end of Verse 12, *"...arise, anoint him, this is he."* David was forgotten by many people, but he wasn't forgotten by

God. Do you know how terrible it must have been to be David? Constantly the last in line to all his siblings, even his Father brought all but him to stand before the Prophet Samuel.

How many of you have felt like the last one picked, the last one to find a happy marriage, the last one to settle into your own home, the last one to feel whole after years of anguish, silently suffering in your own personal hell of anxiety, addiction, and depression? David felt that. David's Father's response to Samuel was essentially, "Well, yeah, there's one more; I guess I could get that one in here, too." His family thought so little of him that they didn't consider him an option. But God. But God considered David. God saw David alone, tending the sheep. God heard David's prayers; God knew David's heart.

When you feel like the last one remembered, please keep in mind that no matter what you are going through, nothing can stop God's anointing on your life. Nothing can stop the Almighty God from remembering you and bringing you to a position you would never have imagined for yourself.

In a later chapter, we will discuss David's conquest of the Philistines and his rise to Kingship. But for now, in this moment, we must revel that David, a lonely shepherd boy, was remembered by the One true God, Who had the power to change his life forever, and He did.

Jesus, in His complete humanity, felt forgotten by God. The night He knew His betrayal and death were coming, He was in the garden with His disciples as the morning hours were closing in on Him. Each of the four gospels has an account of Jesus in the Garden of Gethsemane; however, I feel Mark and Luke have the best descriptions of the anguish He experienced. His human response in each of the gospels is heart-wrenching and arguably the most "relatable" depiction of Jesus's life during His time here on earth.

In Chapter 22 of Luke's Gospel, verses 41-44, *"And He (Jesus) withdrew from them about a stone's throw and knelt down and prayed. Saying, 'Father, if You are willing, remove this cup from Me; yet not My will but (Always) Yours be done.' And there appeared to Him an angel from Heaven, strengthening Him in spirit. And being in agony (of mind), He prayed all the more earnestly and intently, and his sweat became like great clots of blood dropping down upon the ground."*

Luke was a physician. He knew anatomy, and therefore we would expect him to focus more on the medical ramifications of Jesus's anguish, His stress over what His Spirit knew was coming, and His anxiety over the dire circumstances ahead.

How many of you have had physical ailments caused by your anxiety, panic, addiction, and depression? When I was in the throes of my anxiety, even after the panic attacks subsided, I was still in a very toxic living situation. I was left with a constant feeling of dread and nervousness. This nervousness manifested throughout my body and caused some scary side effects, like extreme irritable bowel syndrome; weight just kept piling on without any hope of coming off; my heart would beat irregularly, and I would constantly tremor without knowing how to make it stop.

Bodily reactions are incredibly uncomfortable, and thank goodness, no stranger to our Savior. How comforting to know that when we go through these scary physical experiences, and pray for deliverance, we can rest assured that Jesus has felt the same way. He knows how intense fear and anxiety can be and how horrible the side effects can get, bringing out such terrible reactions to the stressful circumstances in life.

Mark's Gospel gives us a deeper description of what Jesus experienced. Chapter 14:32-37, *"Then they went to a place called Gethsemane, and He said to His disciples, 'Sit down here while I pray.'* (Verse 33) *And He took with Him Peter, and James, and John, and began to be struck with terror and amazement and deeply troubled and depressed.* (Verse 34) *And He said to them, 'My soul is exceedingly sad (overwhelmed with grief) so that it almost kills me! Remain here and keep awake and watching'* (Verse 35) *And going a little farther, He fell on the ground and kept praying that if it were possible the (Fatal) hour might pass from Him.* (Verse 36) *And He was saying, 'Abba (which means) Father, everything is possible for You. Take away this cup from me; yet not what I will, but what You (will)'.* (Verse 37) *And he came back and found them sleeping, and He said to Peter, 'Simon, are you asleep? Have you not the strength to keep awake and watch (with Me for) one hour?'"*

Have you ever been so overrun with fear and anxiety that you thought you would die? Jesus said that his soul was so exceedingly overwhelmed with grief that it felt like it would kill Him. He was struck with terror and depression. Jesus brought three of his best friends with Him to help keep watch for one hour, and while He was pleading with God the Father to let the cup pass from Him, to spare Him, to save

Him from his genuine fears, what did his friends do? They fell asleep.

Jesus not only felt abandoned by God the Father, being left alone in the garden to await His impending betrayal, but when He didn't get the response He wanted from the Father, He went to find His friends, and they were sound asleep. How alone Jesus must have felt!

There was a time during my panic attacks when I would wake up in the middle of the night, my heart racing, and I felt so scared and alone. I would pace around, praying and pleading with God to "let this cup pass" in my own life. I found so much comfort when I read about Jesus in the garden. I related to His overwhelming fear, the overwhelming dread, and anxiety for what was to come, the begging and pleading for the God Who can do anything to please see me, to spare me, to give me the answer I deeply desired, which was to let this situation pass. I understand the turmoil Jesus faced when He went to His friends, who were sound asleep, unaware of the struggle.

In verse 38, Jesus asks them to stay awake and keep watch. (Verse 39) *"He went away again and prayed saying the same words.* (Verse 40) *And again He came back and found them sleeping, for their eyes were very heavy; and they did not know what answer to give Him.* (Verse 41) *And He came back a third time and said to them, 'Are you still sleeping and resting? It's enough (of that)! The hour has come. The Son of Man is betrayed into the hands of sinful men.'* (Verse 42) *'Get up, let us be going! See my betrayer is at hand!'"* Jesus's best friends let Him down three times and left Him alone in His deepest, darkest hour. The hour that Jesus was in His most vulnerable state. The hour that He needed the comfort from His closest friends the most, He was forgotten.

Throughout this intense season of my life, my second husband had little empathy for the panic attacks I struggled to conquer. During the nights of pure panic, I was brushed off by an irritated half-asleep husband and left alone to fend for myself.

During the days that I struggled to go to work and make it through the day, I was called "weak" when I got home. I felt as though I couldn't express any feelings of exhaustion without being ridiculed. I was called "weak" by the man who took vows to protect my heart and love me in sickness and health. Just like Jesus, when the deepest, darkest time of His life arrived, I, too, related to the pain. The one person who was supposed to be closest to me forgot me.

Knowing God could do anything, I would spend my nights pacing and pleading with Him to please help me. Yet night after night, I did not get an answer, which was itself an answer. I knew that I would have to suffer a little longer, that the "cup" wouldn't pass, and I would have to go through with an uncertain date or time of deliverance.

Brothers and sisters, Jesus is incredible. He is what we should strive to be every second of every day. He continued to ask the Father, until the time for asking was up, and then he accepted that the only option He had was to follow through with His Father's will. Doing this takes courage, trust, and, most of all, the incredible faith that He modeled for us during His time on earth. It takes a lot of confidence to continue to do God's work and fulfill His will for your life, especially when you feel you have been forgotten.

He struggled until His very last words on the cross. Matthew 27:46, *"And about the ninth hour (three o'clock) Jesus cried with a loud voice, 'Eli Eli lama sabachthani?'—that is, My God, My God, why have You abandoned Me (leaving Me helpless, forsaking and failing Me in My need)?* (Verse 50) *And Jesus cried again with a loud voice and gave up His Spirit."*

We have a God who understands. When I was a teenager and heard these verses during Easter time, I used to think, "Why would God allow Jesus to be forgotten? Why did those have to be His last words?" It took me a long time to realize that God allowed Jesus to feel forgotten until His last breath so we could have full relatability during the trials we experience.

In life, we will experience real hurt and pain, some of which we won't have a resolution to during our time here on earth. Jesus had to die and go through to be the Sacrificial Lamb for our sins. Seeing His restoration AFTER His last moments of feeling forgotten is so much more important. He was not only remembered but made whole, and through his suffering and passion, we now have hope…hope that can allow us to believe that there is going to be a day when we, too, won't feel forgotten, when we, too, will feel whole and restored by the extraordinary powers of God.

In my early twenties, my first husband and I had just finalized our divorce and were working through a very intense custody battle. I remember dropping my daughter off at her father's house, the house we bought together, the house we were supposed to raise our daughter in together, the place that was once our home.

After dropping her off that Saturday night and being completely emotionally drained, I drove to the nearest Catholic Church and stood in the back. Now I must point out that this was not the church I regularly attended. Although I was raised Catholic, my family went to a different Catholic Church about 35 miles away, so I was essentially a stranger at this particular church. I was so angry with God when I walked up to the church. I remember boiling over with bitterness and resentment towards Him as I stood in the entryway and half-listened to the Mass through the speakers.

The entryway was separate from the main church area, and a wall of glass windows allowed you to see into the church service without having to be in the central area of the church. As I stood there pacing by the windows, one of the younger ushers opened the door to the inside of the church and motioned for me to come in. That man didn't know that behind the glass was just about as close to God as I wanted to be in that moment. It was such a struggle to love God and hate Him simultaneously for completely forgetting me.

I had been a youth group leader, a great student, and all-around good kid. I found myself pregnant in college and rushed to a courthouse wedding with my then-boyfriend to "make the situation right." The marriage lasted a year before he wanted to be single again, leaving me alone trying to raise a child. While I was, in many ways, still a child myself.

I had tried to do the right thing, and yet God, for whatever reason, didn't feel like I deserved to have a husband, a family, and a constant father to help me raise my daughter. No, instead, God left me alone. I tossed all these thoughts as I reluctantly followed the usher into the church. I sat at the very last pew, the farthest away from the altar I could get. I sat there so irate, tossing my angry thoughts around and half listening to the Mass.

As I glanced around, I noticed that EVERYONE was either a couple or a family. Literally everyone in the church. Like, what are the odds of that?! As I looked around, I got increasingly upset staring at the backs of all these "perfect" and "deserving" people whom God clearly loved more than He did me. People, God didn't forget. People He remembered.

This is embarrassing, but I started making up scenarios in my head as I surveyed the people around the church. *I bet he's sleeping with his secretary, and his wife doesn't even know it. I bet that isn't even his kid.* It certainly wasn't my finest moment, but when you get to a place where you feel so forgotten by God, so abandoned, the worst tends to come out.

So, as I am *not* listening to the Priest and wholly focused on judging everyone around me, the Mass finally gets to the time when everyone offers each other the "sign of peace." For those not Catholic, the "sign of peace" is when everyone gets up and hugs or shakes hands, offering peace to one another. Let's keep in mind that I was sitting alone and, therefore, was not offered the sign of peace. Not only was I not physically offered the sign of peace, but no one even turned around to wave (as sometimes they do). How's that for adding fuel to the fire? First, God forgets me, then everyone is a couple or happy family sitting around me, and now all these perfect people don't bother to glance back?

The sign of peace is typically quick. As soon as the thirty seconds is over, everyone kneels as the Priest prepares the altar for communion; what the entire Mass is preparing the congregation for. Once the Priest starts breaking the bread (which in the Catholic Church is the Body of Christ in Eucharist form), everyone is silent, kneeling and preparing to receive communion. It's important to understand exactly where we were when the next moments unfold. As I kneel in my pew, minding my own business, and holding tight to my ever-growing anger, I feel a tap on my shoulder.

I was not happy. I thought, *seriously, what could you possibly want?* I was sure someone was going to ask me to move down to make room in my pew, and I wasn't thrilled in the least. As the entire church was quiet and focused on the Priest preparing the Eucharist, I glanced over with arguably the meanest look I have ever given anyone and stared at the face of a very old and fragile man, who appeared to be one of the ushers in the church. I just stared at him, trying to adjust my extremely vicious stare to something less threatening, when he just smiled and reached out his hand. I didn't know what else to do, so I reached out and took his hand. Cupping my hand between his two hands, he squeezed it tight and said, "Peace be with you."

At this point, I was utterly perplexed and confused because the sign of peace was well over, and NO ONE in the Catholic church deviates from the altar when the Priest is preparing the Eucharist. I stared at him and whispered, "Peace be with you."

He smiled, locked his eyes on my eyes, and said, squeezing my hand, "You know, I always save the best for last." He squeezed my hand one more time and walked away.

I was remembered. God sent someone to remember me. I was picked out specially and remembered at just the right moment for me. I completely broke down in tears. I had been so angry with God, and yet, I knew the stranger's words were true. God didn't forget me; He was preparing me. It was not yet my time, and I was rushing things.

As I was kneeling and looking around the church, tears streamed down my face, my gaze caught the giant cross in the middle of the altar. In the Catholic Church, the cross is considered a Crucifix, which means that Jesus's body is still on the cross, showing the suffering He endured to die for our sins. As I scanned Jesus on the cross, my anger turned into sadness and then turned into surrender. I started praying and told God I had tried to handle everything on my own and accomplished nothing but being alone, hurt, and full of anger.

I told God that day, from that moment on, we were doing this together no matter what came my way. I ensured that God understood I was still angry and hurt, but if I had to do life with or without Him, no matter what came my way, I would rather do it with Him. I left the church that day with a glimmer of hope that no matter what my life looked like, no matter what situation I was coming up against, I had a God Who, in the words of that very old, sweet man, would "save the best for last."

So, remember, if you are struggling and feel as though God has forgotten you, remember that in their very old age, Abraham and Sarah were given a miracle. After years of torment and embarrassment, Hannah was given a son. While everyone else was being considered, God saw David and remembered him, anointing him to be a great King, a man after God's own heart. And last but not least, Jesus, through betrayal and agony, felt the pain of being forgotten and yet modeled how to keep the faith, no matter what our earthly circumstances say. Forgotten can be God's fancy way of saying, "Not yet, but soon." As you continue on in your journey of healing and conquering your panic attacks, your depression, your addiction, and your anxiety, I pray you will remember to relate with the men and women who have gone before you, paving the way for deliverance, wholeness, and remembrance that will come, not in your time, but in God's perfect time, which He has hand-picked just for you.

# CHAPTER 11: PERSPECTIVE

*"Set your mind on things above, not on things on the earth."*
–Colossians 3:2 (NKJV)

What do you do when you are in the depths of a battle and feel the enemy is so large, so powerful, you freeze in terror? You watch yourself shrink while the problems continue to grow and consume you, leaving you helpless. Many times, in life, your anxieties, fears, and depression will seem magnified. You will feel trapped in a web of emotions, unable to break free.

Remember, perspective is everything if you want to conquer your deepest fears. The words we use can either bring life or death into a situation. (AMP, Proverbs 18:21), *"Death and life are in the power of the tongue, And those who love it and indulge it will eat its fruit and bear the consequences of their words."* Ouch. So, the Bible plainly tells us that our words are powerful, and the words we choose, whether negative or positive, will affect our life.

When we give into our emotions and speak words reflecting on how our emotions make us feel, we give power to those emotions. There were so many times that I "felt" the emotion of fear, the emotion of panic, and depression that all I could do was speak about it, think about it, and talk about how terrible it made me feel. My words would reinforce the emotion, and the emotion would grow stronger from the words I spoke. It was a vicious cycle that kept my spirit in captivity.

Breaking the cycle is extremely hard. The old saying, "Fake it until you make it," comes into play here. Once I realized what I was doing and how damaging my words were to my life, I made a very conscious effort to speak life back into the darkness that was consuming me. I am not going to lie; there were so many times when I would be shaking, pacing, and physically sick to my stomach over my anxiety as I said, "Lord, thank you for this emotion. I know you are more powerful and can see me through it. Where You are, there is peace and happiness, and I feel joy every day."

Lies. I did NOT feel joy every day, and certainly not peace or happiness; HOWEVER, I needed to remind myself that our emotions and thoughts are two different entities. You can have an emotion, but you are not obligated to give in to what that emotion is telling you.

When faced with reckless emotions that come at us from all directions, we are given the opportunity to decide to react with negativity or positivity. We can either see the jumbled up, disgusting mess in front of us and focus on every emotion that welcomes itself into our mind or we can see the outcome as Christ claims over our lives, knowing that His words are final and always in our best interest.

Speaking life into a dead situation seems helpless, hopeless, and pointless. It is much easier to feel bad, accept the feeling, harp on the feeling, and repeat. Breaking free takes time. It takes dedication and determination, especially when you don't see progress immediately. It took me months to re-wire my mind to truly believe the life-giving words I was speaking over my life. Your emotions and words won't always line up. Still, if you persistently keep pressing forward, you will slowly but surely see victory. Your perspective will change, and you will find yourself believing the words you struggled so hard to speak and believe at the beginning of your journey.

King David knew the importance and power of words:

**Psalm 27 of David (NIV):**

1 *"The Lord is my light and my salvation—*
*whom shall I fear?*
*The Lord is the stronghold of my life—*
*of whom shall I be afraid?*

[2] *When the wicked advance against me*
*to devour me,*
*it is my enemies and my foes*
*who will stumble and fall.*
[3] *Though an army besiege me,*
*my heart will not fear;*
*though war break out against me,*
*even then, I will be confident.*
[4] *One thing I ask from the Lord,*
*this only do I seek:*
*that I may dwell in the house of the Lord*
*all the days of my life,*
*to gaze on the beauty of the Lord*
*and to seek Him in His temple.*
[5] *For in the day of trouble*
*He will keep me safe in His dwelling;*
*He will hide me in the shelter of His sacred tent*
*and set me high upon a rock.*
[6] *Then my head will be exalted*
*above the enemies who surround me;*
*at His sacred tent, I will sacrifice with shouts of joy;*
*I will sing and make music to the Lord.*
[7] *Hear my voice when I call, Lord;*
*be merciful to me and answer me.*
[8] *My heart says of you, "Seek his face!"*
*Your face, Lord, I will seek.*
[9] *Do not hide Your face from me,*
*do not turn Your servant away in anger;*
*You have been my helper.*
*Do not reject me or forsake me,*
*God, my Savior.*
[10] *Though my father and mother forsake me,*
*the Lord will receive me.*
[11] *Teach me your way, Lord;*
*lead me in a straight path*
*because of my oppressors.*
[12] *Do not turn me over to the desire of my foes,*
*for false witnesses rise up against me,*
*spouting malicious accusations.*

*13 I remain confident of this:*
*I will see the goodness of the Lord*
*in the land of the living.*
*14 Wait for the Lord;*
*be strong and take heart*
*and wait for the Lord."*

*"I remain confident in this; I will see the goodness of the Lord in the land of the living."* David knew real fear. He also knew the power of words and the strength in speaking God's provision and authority over his life at all times. When David was just a young boy, King Saul requested his presence to play the lyre for him when he felt that the evil spirits were upon him. King Saul became so fond of David that he made David his armor-bearer.

Not long after David's promotion, the Philistine army rose against the Israelites. 1 Samuel Chapter 17 Verse 3-11, *"And the Philistines stood on a mountain on one side and Israel stood on a mountain on the other side, with the valley between them.* (Verse 4) *And a champion went out of the camp of the Philistines named Goliath of Gath, whose height was six cubits and a span (almost 10 feet).* (Verse 5) *And he had a bronze helmet on his head and wore a coat of mail, and the coat weighed 5,000 shekels of bronze.* (Verse 6) *He had bronze shin armor on his legs and a bronze javelin across his shoulders.* (Verse 7) *And the shaft of his spear was like a weaver's beam; his spear's head weighed 600 shekels of iron. And a shield-bearer went before him.* (Verse 8) *Goliath stood and shouted to the ranks of Israel, 'Why have you come out to draw up for battle? Am I, not a Philistine, and are you not servants of Saul? Choose a man for yourselves and let him come down to me.* (Verse 9) *If he is able to fight with me and kill me, then we will be your servants; but if I prevail against him and kill him, then you shall be our servants and serve us.'* (Verse 10) *And the Philistine said, 'I defy the ranks of Israel this day; give me a man, that we may fight together.'* (Verse 11) *When Saul and all Israel heard those words of the Philistine, they were dismayed and greatly afraid."*

How intimidating Goliath must have been! In life, we will face many "Goliaths," whether it's anxiety, addiction, depression, a panic that won't let up, a custody battle that seems never-ending, financial stress that has left you living paycheck to paycheck, a rebellious teenager, a divorce that is dragged out and has left you completely depleted of everything you once knew. Goliath can take many different forms in our lives; however, the image of intimidation tends to be a common factor when facing whichever "Goliath" is in front of you at any given moment. It's daunting to face a situation or emotion that you feel no control over. Seeing a big, evil, scary giant staring you down is terrifying as you feel completely helpless.

I love that the Bible clearly describes the armor Goliath was suited up with. When satan comes at us, attacking in the most intimidating way possible, it can feel as though we are so weak and so vulnerable while he is so strong and powerful. It feels like our fears are presented to us in such detail that we cannot focus on anything else. It is easy to get wrapped up in the emotions of the battle rather than the strategy of war. Verse 11 tells us that Saul and all of Israel were "dismayed and greatly afraid." Their perspective was on the Giant before them rather than on what their God could do for them. Skipping to Verse 16, *"The Philistine came out morning and evening, presenting himself for forty days."*

FORTY DAYS. How many days have your fears, your anxieties, your addiction, and your depression presented themselves to you? Day after day, being presented with the bondages of your past and the helplessness and hopelessness of your situation.

Satan will come at you day in and day out until you decide you will not take it anymore. Until you take that stand, brothers and sisters, the Goliath you are facing will be brought to your attention until it wears you down, beats you down, and leaves you gasping for air as you barely survive each day. As the days go on, your fear grows, and your anxieties become affirmed and fixed as you slowly lose your self-worth and value as a child of God. (Verse 23), *"As they talked, behold, Goliath, the champion, the Philistine of Gath, came forth from the Philistine ranks and spoke the same words as before, and David heard him."* The words did not change. The threatening words from the last 40 days stayed the same; what changed was who heard them.

Let me say that again, *what changed, was who heard them.* You do not have to be the same person today that you were yesterday. The fears that held you back yesterday do not have to have control or power over your life any longer. The more time you take to build your relationship with God, the quicker you will transition from feeling defeated to experiencing an overwhelming victory.

David knew who he was in God. He knew the power of God, and therefore when the threatening, terrifying words came out yet again amongst the Israelites, David heard them; however, his focus was not on the damage this Goliath could do but on what his God could do despite the unfavorable circumstance.

There's a saying I love that says, "David never really knew Goliath's strength; he was too focused on God's." How incredible to be able to face our fears solely focused on the strength of our God. (Verse 26), *"And David said to the men standing by him, 'What shall be done for the man who kills this Philistine and takes away the reproach from Israel? For who is this uncircumcised Philistine that he should defy the armies of the living God?'"* David wasn't having it. He heard the words, accepted the words, and went right into what God could do to purge this unclean man from their midst. (Verse 28), *"Now Eliab, his (David's) eldest brother, heard what he said to the men; and Eliab's anger was kindled against David, and he said, 'Why did you come here? With whom have you left those few sheep in the wilderness? I know your presumption and evilness of heart; for you came down that you might see the battle.'"*

David was faced with Eliab's narrow perspective of viewing him only as a small shepherd boy. When you are trying to break a bondage, an addiction, a pattern that has been presenting itself to you day in and day out, you will, unfortunately, have resistance come against you. As it was with David, the opposition, judgment, and limited perspectives will often come from people who are supposed to care about and love you the most.

When others can't see the plan God has for you, it can make your breakthrough that much harder. David's brother had no problem pointing out that David was a shepherd and insinuated that with his sheep is where he should be, instead of on the battlefield where the "strong men" were. Their disbelief that you can overcome a situation they may not understand or have been struggling to conquer themselves without luck can make you question your faith and abilities.

When I started writing this book, my second husband would flip-flop between being supportive and discouraging. On the days where I seemed to be holding it together, he would be on the "supportive" side, but then there were days when I would be an anxious mess writing the book and would literally have my anxiety medicine sitting next to me as I poured over the Bible, struggling to write my next chapter. On those days, he would make comments like, "How are you going to help people with anxiety if you can't fix yourself first?"

Comments like those left me feeling defeated and questioning my purpose. In all honestly, it was a valid question… hurtful but valid. I didn't know how I would help people while I was in the throes of panic, desperately writing this book. Still, I knew in my deepest inner self that this was a book God wanted to use to help others, and knowing that was enough for me. I got to the point where I would respond, "Well, if I'm still panicking, then the book isn't finished yet."

It is so important to not let the attacks from the enemy take a foothold and shake your foundation. Standing firm on everything God promises is the only way to have complete victory in your life. (Verses 32-33), *"David said to Saul, 'Let no man's heart fail because of this Philistine; your servant will go out and fight with him.' And Saul said to David, 'You are not able to go to fight against this Philistine. You are only an adolescent, and he has been a warrior from his youth.'"* David, again being told why he can't do something, based now on Saul's limited perspective, explains to Saul that during his time shepherding, he killed both a lion and a bear, and the same fate will come to Goliath because he has defied the armies of the living God. (Verse 37), *"David said, 'The Lord Who delivered me out of the paw of the lion and out of the paw of the bear, He will deliver me out of the hand of this Philistine.' And Saul said to David, 'Go, and the Lord will be with you!'"*

Confidence—David had confidence that the Lord, who had seen him through other scary circumstances, would see him through this next one, for there were no limitations on what the living God of Israel could do. (Verse 38), *"Then Saul clothed David with his armor; he put a bronze helmet on his head and clothed him with a coat of mail.* (Verse 39) *And David girded his sword over his armor. Then he tried to go but could not, for he was not used to it. And David said to Saul, 'I cannot go with these, for I am not used to them,' and David took them off.* (Verse 40) *Then he took his staff in his hand and chose five smooth stones out of the brook and put them in his shepherd's bag, in his pouch, and his sling was in his hand, and he drew near the Philistine."*

The world will tell us how to handle our anxiety, our depression, our addiction and our panic. If you have struggled, even for a little while, you will soon realize everyone has an antidote for your problem. David knew he could defeat Goliath; however, he was still being told what to wear, what to take, and how to do it. Just like David, we must realize that although there are excellent and healthy coping mechanisms to help us through our problems, we must never forget that we have the Living God who will needs to be put at the center of our problems. Focusing on His strength instead of the scare tactics of the enemy will keep our perspective on the goodness of God. (Verse 43-49), *"And the Philistine said to David, 'Am I a dog, that you should come to me with sticks?' And the Philistine cursed David by his gods.* (Verse 44) *The Philistine said to David, 'Come to me, and I will give your flesh to the birds of the air and the beasts of the field.'* (Verse 45) *Then David said to the Philistine, 'You come to me with a sword, a spear, and a javelin, but I come to you in the name of the Lord of hosts, the God of the ranks of Israel, Whom you have defied.* (Verse 46) *This day the Lord will deliver you into my hand, and I will smite you and cut off your head. And I will give the corpses of the army of the Philistines this day to the birds of the air and the wild beasts of the earth, that all the earth may know there is a God in Israel.* (Verse 47) *And all this assembly shall know that the Lord saves, not with sword and spear; for the battle is the Lord's, and He will give you into our hands.'* (Verse 48) *When the Philistine came forward to meet David, David ran quickly toward the battle line to meet the Philistine.* (Verse 49) *David put his hand into his bag and took out a stone and slung it, and it struck the Philistine, sinking into his forehead, and he fell on his face to the earth."*

David ran quickly toward the battle line. There wasn't hesitation, wavering, or second-guessing. When dealing with an enemy attack, we need to act just as David did. We need to grasp onto everything the Lord promises and run straight at our adversary, knowing that the Lord is greater, stronger, and mightier than anything thrown our way. David spoke back to the Goliath, staring him down. The scary, threatening words Goliath spoke to shake David up; David spoke right back to him, following up with his adamant proclamation that the battle was not his but the Lord's.

Brothers and sisters, you are children of the Most High God! Any battle you face is not yours alone to fight. You have a Heavenly Father who always goes before you and stands before you as a shield when the enemy attacks. During the times when you are so overwhelmed with panic, fear, and worry, remember David—remember his faith, his steadfastness. Remember his reliance, believing in the Lord to defeat Goliath. Think about the unwavering faith that brought victory over the Philistines, freeing Israel from the Goliath that presented himself day after day for forty days. Although small, David had God's mighty power inside of him. We are all given the power to fight against the attacks that come against us, allowing each of us to become conquerors through Christ, slaying every Goliath that comes our way.

Gideon, another great man of God, was working in the wheat fields when an Angel of the Lord appeared to him. (Judges 6:11-16), *"Now the Angel of the Lord came and sat under the oak at Ophrah, which belonged to Joash the Abiezrite, and his son Gideon was beating wheat in the winepress to hide it from the Midianites.* (Verse 12) *And the Angel of the Lord appeared to him and said to him, 'The Lord is with you, you mighty man of (fearless) courage.'* (Verse 13) *And Gideon said to him, 'O sir, if the Lord is with us, why is all this befallen us? And where are all His wonderous works of which our fathers told us, saying, "Did not the Lord bring us up from Egypt?" But now the Lord has forsaken us and given us into the hand of the Midian.'* (Verse 14) *The Lord turned to him and said, 'Go in this your might, and you shall save Israel from the hand of the Midian. Have I not sent you?'* (Verse 15) *Gideon said to him, 'Oh Lord, how can I deliver Israel? Behold, my clan is the poorest in Manasseh, and I am the least in my father's house.'* (Verse 16) *The Lord said to him, 'Surely I will be with you, and you shall smite the Midianites as one man.'"*

God sent an angel to find Gideon, while he was executing his regular day-to-day chores. When God has a specific purpose for your life, He will always meet you exactly where you are, usually when you least expect it. Gideon recognized the problem with his people and the strain of being under Midian rule; however, when the Lord sent him forward to deliver the Israelites, Gideon immediately mentioned that he was from a very poor clan and was the least in his father's house. Gideon, just like David, was the least in his father's house, yet God saw an incredible potential in him. Gideon's perspective was one of helplessness and hopelessness; God's perspective of Gideon was one of a warrior, a deliverer, and a fearless man of courage.

How often do we focus on everything holding us back from the incredible potential God has in store for us? How often is the perspective of our past or current status used as an excuse as to why we aren't qualified for the work God anointed us for? When God called Gideon, He didn't see the circumstances surrounding him; He saw his heart. Let me say that one more time. *God did not see the circumstances surrounding Gideon; He saw his heart.*

So often in life, we are consumed with the dread and fear surrounding us that we can't see past our own problems. Thank goodness we have a God with a different vantage point. A God who sees the potential in our hearts and not the failings of our flesh. Over the next few verses, Gideon asks the Lord to give him a sign to prove that he is indeed speaking with the Lord. (Verse 23), *"The Lord said to him, 'Peace be to you, do not fear; you shall not die.'"*

Gideon received a sign from the Lord, a command not to fear, and a promise of survival. In life, we will face many different challenges, most of which will spark fear and uncertainty. During these times, it is crucial to keep our perspective not on what we see around us but rather on what God sees for us and in us.

There have been many times in my life when I felt like I had made too many mistakes for God to even think of using me to help others. When our mind gets muddied with words of defeat, it is much easier to retreat back to the feelings of self-doubt than to push forward in faith into the unknown. (Verse 24), *"Then Gideon built an altar there to the Lord and called it, The Lord is Peace. To this day, it still stands in Ophrah, which belongs to the Abiezrites."* Gideon heard the word of God, believed the word of God, and built an altar to be a constant reminder of the promises of God.

This is such an important life lesson. We must listen, believe, and live as though the promises of God are true every day. The Lord then commands Gideon to take his father's second bull and tear down the altar of Baal that his father had built and cut down the Asherah. Then he is told to construct a new altar to the Lord, burn the second bull as an offering, and use the Asherah for firewood. Gideon obeys the Lord but, out of fear, takes ten of his own men and completes the Lord's task under cover of darkness.

The next day, the men of the city saw that the altar of Baal was destroyed and that the Asherah was cut down beside it; they searched around the city and discovered that Gideon, the son of Joash, was responsible. (Verse 30) *"Then the men of the city commanded Joash, 'Bring out your son that he may die, for he has pulled down the altar of Baal and cut down the Asherah beside it.'"* Joash tells the crowd to let Baal contend for himself and calls his son Gideon, Jererubbal, which means, "Let Baal contend against him because he had pulled down the altar." Gideon gets word of this and immediately sends messengers from four different locations to come help deliver Israel. He then asks God for a sign to prove that He will truly deliver Israel by his hand, as He had promised.

How many times in life do we read the promises of God and then doubt that they will come to fruition? When we believe the promises of God are for everyone else but couldn't possibly be meant for us. (Verse 37) *"Behold, I will put a fleece of wool on the threshing floor. If there is dew on the fleece only and it is dry on all the ground, then I shall know that You will deliver Israel by my hand, as You have said."* (Verse 38*) "And it was so. When he rose early next morning and squeezed the dew out of the fleece, he wrung from it a bowlful of water.* (Verse 39) *And Gideon said to God, 'Let not your anger be kindled against me, and I will speak but this once. Let me make trial only this once with the fleece. I pray you; let it now be dry only upon the fleece and upon all the ground let there be dew.'* (Verse 40) *And God did so that night, for it was dry on the fleece only, and there was dew on all the ground."* Starting in Chapter 7, Gideon and all of the men who were with him to fight, arose to encamp beside the springs of Harod, leaving the Midianites just north of where they were. (Verse 2), *"The Lord said to Gideon, 'The people who are with you are too many for Me to give the Midianites into their hands, lest Israel boast about themselves against Me, saying, "My own hand has delivered me."'"*

I love that the Lord says these words to Gideon. A lot of times in life, we want to feel fully prepared for the battle we are facing. At this point, Gideon is probably feeling "in control" of the situation with his large army of 32,000 men. The fact that the Lord tells him that there are too many people probably shook Gideon to the core. He now has to make a very tough decision to either listen to the Lord and let some men go or push forward with the men he has in order to feel comforted and in control as he prepares for battle.

In life, we are faced with many situations where we can either listen to God's instruction for our life or push on with how we feel and what makes us comfortable. (Verse 3), *"So now proclaim in the ears of the men, saying, 'Whoever is fearful and trembling, let him turn back and depart from Mount Gilead.' And 22,000 of the men returned, but 10,000 remained.* (Verse 4) *And the Lord said to Gideon, 'The men are still too many; bring them down to the water, and I will test them for you there. And he of whom I say to you, "This man shall go with you," shall go with you; and he of whom I say to you, "This man shall not go with you," shall not go.'* (Verse 5) *So he brought the men down to the water, and the Lord said to Gideon, 'Everyone who laps up the water with his tongue as a dog laps it, you shall set by himself, likewise, everyone who bows down on his knees to drink.'* (Verse 6) *And the number of those who lapped, putting their hand to their mouth, was 300, but all the rest of the people bowed down upon their knees to drink water.* (Verse 7) *And the Lord said to Gideon, 'With the 300 men who lapped, I will deliver you, and give the Midianites into your hand. Let all the others return every man to his home.'"*

God removed everyone from Gideon until he was left with a very small and uncomfortable number of warriors to fight with. Sometimes in life, the very things that give us comfort and security are removed by God until there is nothing left but our faith to lean on.

In my own life, there were many times when I was left without a home, without a job, and without a husband, left to rely solely on God and the faith that He would see me through impossible situations. Gideon's army went from 32,000 to 300, leaving him with only his faith in God to carry out the task at hand. (Verse 8*) "So the people took provisions and their trumpets in their hands, and he sent all the rest of Israel, every man to his home and retained those 300 men. And the host of Midian was below him in the valley.* (Verse 9) *That same night the Lord said to Gideon, 'Arise, go down against their camp, for I have given it into your hand.* (Verse 10) *But if you fear to go down, go with Purah your servant down to the camp* (Verse 11) *And you shall hear what they say, and afterward, your hands shall be strengthened to go down against the camp.' Then he went down with Purah, his servant, to the outposts of the camp of the armed men.* (Verse 12) *And the Midianites and the Amalekites and all the sons of the east lay along the valley like locusts for multitude; and their camels were without number as the sand on the seashore for multitude."* I don't think it's a coincidence that God had Gideon send all of the men but the remaining 300 home, and then <u>the same night</u>, send Gideon to the camp to take it over.

We have a very thoughtful God who knows our humanity and understands our fears. I am confident that God knew that if He'd had Gideon wait a few days to attack, the anxiety and panic of only having 300 men would have weighed on him, weakening his faith. Thank goodness we have an on-time God! A God who always has our best interest and understands our humanity. The Lord tells Gideon that the Midianites will be given into his hand; however, the Lord also allows Gideon the opportunity to go down with his servant to listen to what the Midianites are saying, to reassure him, and strengthen him for the fight. Gideon chose to go down with his servant to listen to the army before attacking. On his way down, Gideon leaves his 300 men and comes across a ginormous Midianite army.

How many times in life do we trust God and then turn around to see a giant wall of fear right in front of us. I can only imagine how shocked Gideon was when he saw the Midianites and Amalekites and all the sons of the East lying along the valley, in a number too numerous to count. Right after, he sent all but 300 men home!

God will certainly put us in circumstances where we are tested and tried by faith in order to see how far we will go to trust and believe in Him and His promises. (Verse 13) *"When Gideon arrived, behold, a man was telling a dream to his comrade. And he said, Behold, 'I dreamed a dream, and behold, a cake of barley bread tumbled into the camp of Midian and came to the tent and struck it so that it fell, and turned it upside down so that the tent lay flat.'"* (Verse 14) *And his comrade replied, 'This is nothing else but the sword of Gideon, son of Joash, a man of Israel. Into his hand, God has given Midian and all the host.'* (Verse 15) *When Gideon heard the telling of the dream and its interpretation, he worshipped and returned to the camp of Israel and said, 'Arise, for the Lord has given into your hand the host of Midian.'* (Verse 16) *And he divided the 300 men into three companies, and he put into the hands of all of them trumpets and empty pitchers, with torches inside the pitchers.* (Verse 17) *And he said to them, 'Look at me, then do likewise. When I come to the edge of the camp, do as I do.* (Verse 18) *When I blow the trumpet, I and all who are with me, then you blow the trumpets also on every side of the all the camp and shout, For the Lord and for Gideon!"* (Verse 19) *So Gideon and the 100 men who were with him came to the outskirts of the camp at the beginning of the middle watch, when the guards had just been changed, and they blew the trumpets and smashed the pitchers that were in their hands.* (Verse 20) *And the three companies blew the trumpets and shattered the pitchers, holding the torches in their left hands, and in their right hands the trumpets to blow (leaving no chance to use swords), and they cried, 'The sword for the Lord and Gideon!'* (Verse 21) *They stood every man in his place round about the camp, and all the (Midianite) army ran – they cried out and fled.* (Verse 22) *When (Gideon's men) blew the 300 trumpets, the Lord set every (Midianites) sword against his comrade and against all the army, and the army fled as far as Beth-shittah toward Zererah, as far as the border Abel-meholah by Tabbath."*

God knew that Gideon would overhear the dream interpretation and be strengthened in faith enough to fight for Israel. Knowing that he was severely understaffed with soldiers, Gideon kept believing in God's promise that nothing was impossible with help from the Lord. He devised a plan and stayed the course, despite the extreme disadvantage.

Brothers and sisters, when we know the promises of God and step out in faith, we need to stand firm, even when the situation seems less than favorable. We know that Jesus left His peace with us, therefore, when the anxieties of life pile up, we must separate our emotions from truth and trust God. Just like the angel called Gideon a "Mighty man of fearless courage," we must also believe in the name that the Lord has given each and every one of us as sons and daughters of the Most High God.

We, too, have been chosen for a purpose, hand selected by God to do great and wonderful things. Just like Gideon, it doesn't matter what happened in your past, where you came from, or what you lack. The only perspective that matters is from the Most High God, Who calls each of us by name and not just any name, but a new name, not based on what we are, but on who He sees us to be.

One of my favorite people in the New Testament is good ol' Blind Bartimaeus. Luke 18:35-43 gives the entire account of Bartimaeus's healing; his name is presented to us in Mark's Gospel, but for purposes in this book, we will stick with Luke's interpretation since he was the physician. (Verse 35) *"As He (Jesus) came near to Jericho, it occurred that a blind man was sitting by the roadside begging.* (Verse 36) *And hearing a crowd going by, he asked what it meant.* (Verse 37) *They told him, 'Jesus of Nazareth is passing by.'"* Now let's keep the context. Bartimaeus was blind and by all accounts had probably been blind since birth, always relying on others to "see" for him. Even in verse 37, he is told by the other people standing by what is happening around him. Bartimaeus could not physically see; however, his spirit, his soul, could see, and he internally believed in the power and ability of Jesus. (Verse 38) *"And he shouted, saying, 'Jesus, Son of David, take pity and have mercy on me!'* (Verse 39) *But those who were in front reproved him, telling him to keep quiet; yet he screamed and shrieked so much more, 'Son of David, take pity and have mercy on me!'"*

Bartimaeus was told to be quiet; he was made to feel as though his request wasn't worthy enough for Jesus of Nazareth, that somehow Blind Bartimaeus would be bothering this very important man. The faith and spiritual sight Bartimaeus had to continue shouting for the Lord is precisely how we need to be. He knew that his circumstance would not change unless he met the One Who had the ability to change it. (Verse 40), *"Then Jesus stood still and ordered that he be led to Him; and when he came near, Jesus asked him* (Verse 41) *'What do you want me to do for you?' He said, 'Lord, let me receive my sight!'* (Verse 42) *And Jesus said to him, 'Receive your sight! Your faith has healed you.'* (Verse 43) *And instantly he received his sight and began to follow Jesus, recognizing, praising, and honoring God; and all the people, when they saw it, praised God."*

Jesus stood still. How incredible that when we shout to the Lord with every ounce of desperation, believing that from the perspective of Jesus, we can be healed and made new, Jesus stands still. He waits, He listens, and He tends to the very urgent need that we present. Bartimaeus didn't let the crowd's perspective sway his words when shouting to Jesus and believing for a miracle. He didn't believe their remarks which were likely harsh reminders of his helpless condition and pathetic state of being a beggar. He kept his perspective on Jesus and on what he knew could be accomplished with a lot of perseverance and a little bit of faith.

Zacchaeus was a very wealthy chief tax collector who wanted to see Jesus. Luke 19:1-10, *"And (Jesus) entered Jericho and was passing through it.* (Verse 2) *And there was a man called Zacchaeus, a chief tax collector, and (he was) rich.* (Verse 3) *And he was trying to see Jesus, which One He was, but he could not on account of the crowd, because he was small in stature.* (Verse 4) *So, he ran on ahead and climbed up in a sycamore tree in order to see Him, for He was about to pass that way.* (Verse 5) *And when Jesus reached the place, He looked up and said to him, 'Zacchaeus, hurry and come down; for I must stay at your house today.'* (Verse 6) *So he hurried and came down, and he received and welcomed Him joyfully.* (Verse 7) *And when the people saw it, they all muttered among themselves and indignantly complained, 'He has gone in to be the guest of and lodge with a man who is devoted to sin and preeminently a sinner.'* (Verse 8) *So then Zacchaeus stood up and solemnly declared to the Lord, 'See, Lord, the half of my goods I give to the poor, and if I have cheated anyone out of anything, I restore four times as much.'* (Verse 9) *And Jesus said to him, 'Today is salvation come to this household, since Zacchaeus too is a son of Abraham.* (Verse 10) *For the Son of Man came to seek and to save that which was lost.'"*

Zacchaeus was a sinner with a problem. How many of us can relate to Zacchaeus? In life, we make choices that, by all accounts, should keep us separated from God. We choose lifestyles and make decisions that go against the Christian principles God has directed us to follow. Zacchaeus spent his entire life cheating people out of money in order to live an extremely lavish lifestyle.

How many times have we made decisions to benefit ourselves, not caring about what those decisions will do to the others around us? When Jesus came to town, Zacchaeus wanted to see Jesus, despite his lifestyle. He was willing to put aside embarrassment and judgment just so he could see Jesus. Jesus knew Zacchaeus's heart and sought him. The crowd's perspective was judgment and ridicule, seeing Zacchaeus as the greedy tax collector. Jesus's perspective saw a man who made mistakes yet still did everything he could to be near Him.

I believe Jesus called Zacchaeus down from the tree because He saw his determination. The others gathering in the streets might have been "more holy"; however, Zacchaeus fought against his short stature and did everything he could to be near God. As we go through struggles, we must always fight against them and find a way to re-route in order to be closer to God. Just like Zacchaeus, we must ask for forgiveness from our sins and choose to be made new through our encounter with Jesus.

The woman with the issue of blood is one of my favorite women in the Bible. Mark 5:21, *"And when Jesus had recrossed in the boat to the other side, a great throng gathered about Him, and He was at the lakeshore.* (Verse 22) *Then one of the rulers of the synagogue came up, Jairus by name; and seeing Him, he prostrated himself at His feet.* (Verse 23) *And begged Him earnestly, saying, 'My little daughter is at the point of death. Come and lay Your hands on her, so that she may be healed and live.'* (Verse 24) *And Jesus went with him; and a great crowd kept following Him and pressed Him from all sides (as almost to suffocate Him)."*

Ok, pause here. So, Jesus had just arrived back to shore and was immediately met with a large crowd. Jairus, an important ruler, came up to Him, begging for healing for his daughter, who was dying. Jesus immediately follows Jairus to his house when the crowd starts closing in on Him from all sides. Jairus's perspective was on the healer, fully trusting Jesus to save his child. (Verse 25) *"And there was a woman who had a flow of blood for twelve years.* (Verse 26) *And who had endured much suffering under (the hands of) many physicians and had spent all that she had and was no better but instead grew worse."*

I always like to reference Luke's Gospel when it comes to medical situations in the Bible. Luke, as mentioned previously, was a physician and tended to have a little more medical insight. Luke 8:43, *"And a woman who had suffered from a flow of blood for twelve years and had spent all her living upon physicians and could not be healed by anyone."*

OK, facts established: 1) she had an issue for twelve years. How many years have you had your constant, persistent, ever-present issue of anxiety, depression, or addiction? How many days, months, and years have you struggled, day in and day out, without hope for a cure? Most importantly, how often have you referred to yourself as your problem?

The woman with the issue of blood had a name. Yet no one seems to know her name or even cared to acknowledge it in scripture. She is known purely by her issue. How many of you feel like you are defined solely by your issue? Sometimes we get so consumed with our anxiety, panic, addiction and depression that we only see ourselves as a broken, worthless mess. That identity overrides anything and everything that Christ says about us.

Fact 2) She could not be healed by anyone. When you are in the depths of depression, and addiction, consumed with anxiety and the hopelessness of panic, the thought of being cured is so far away it almost sounds easier to hit the lottery. The woman spent everything she had and was still coming up empty.

A lot of times in life, we look for healing in everything but Jesus. The medications help, exercise helps, but nothing compares to the healing touch of our Savior, which the woman with the issue of blood realized after years of exhausting all other viable options. (Verse 27), *"She had heard the reports concerning Jesus, and she came up behind Him in the throng and touched His garment."* (Verse 28) *For she kept saying, 'If I only touch His garments, I shall be restored to health.'"*

The woman's perspective focused solely on Jesus and His ability to heal her. There was a massive crowd around Him, and she snuck in to just touch the hem of his garment. How powerful her faith must have been for just the dirty hem of His garment to be enough for her healing.

So right now, at this moment, we have Jairus going up to Jesus, face to face, and making a request. His perspective believed that Jesus could save his dying daughter. Then we have the woman with the issue of blood, who was quite the opposite of important Jairus. She was a nobody who was desperate for her own healing. Her perspective believed that she only needed to touch the hem of His clothing to be healed and sneak up like a thief to grab the scraps she could get.

(Verse 29) *"And immediately her flow of blood was dried up at the source, and (suddenly) she felt in her body that she was healed of her ailment.* (Verse 30) *And Jesus, recognizing in Himself that the power proceeding from Him had gone forth, turned around immediately in the crowd and said, 'Who touched my clothes?'*

(Verse 31) *And the disciples kept saying to Him, 'You see the crowd pressing hard around You from all sides, and You ask, 'Who touched Me?'* (Verse 32) *Still, He kept looking around to see her who had done it.* (Verse 33) *But the woman, knowing what had been done for her, though alarmed and frightened and trembling, fell down before Him and told Him the whole truth.* (Verse 34) *And He said to her, 'Daughter, your faith has restored you to health. Go in peace and be continually healed and freed from your disease.'"*

Jesus stops on the way to heal Jairus' daughter and searches for the woman who was known solely by her issue. He seeks until he finds her, and then He leaves her with a new identity. On His way to heal a very important man's daughter, Jesus reminds the woman with the issue of blood that she, too, is an important daughter of the Most High God. Jesus stops everything He is doing in order to call the woman back and tell her that His perspective of her is one of a worthy and valuable Daughter. She leaves Jesus not only healed but with a new identity.

(Verse 35) *"While He was still speaking, there came some from the ruler's house, who said (to Jairus), 'Your daughter has died. Why bother and distress the teacher any longer?'"* I wonder if Jairus' perspective changed at this moment. He had just witnessed a woman sneak in, receive healing and be given a new name of Daughter, delaying Jesus from getting to his own daughter faster. He hears the news that his daughter has died, and the firm belief that Jesus could save her might have dwindled out in those moments.

How many times have you begged God for healing in your life, only to see someone else healed first? How frustrating it is when you are at your most desperate breaking point, and all you can see is the deliverance and answered prayers of those around you. Sometimes it feels as though you aren't as important as one of God's other children. (Verse 36) *"Overhearing but ignoring what they said, Jesus said to the ruler of the synagogue, 'Do not be seized with alarm and struck with fear; only keep on believing.'"* Jesus's perspective stayed focused on what He knew He could accomplish with God, not on the perspective of those who came from Jairus's house. (Verse 37) *"And he permitted no one to accompany Him except Peter and James and John, the brother of James.* (Verse 38) *When they arrived at the house of the ruler of the synagogue, He looked at the tumult and the people weeping and wailing loudly.* (Verse 39) *And when He had gone in, He said to them, 'Why do you make an uproar and weep? The little girl is not dead but is sleeping.'* (Verse 40) *And they laughed and jeered at Him. But He put them all out, and, taking the child's father and mother and those who were with Him, He went in where the little girl was lying."*

Jesus kept His focus on the healing; He removed everyone in the room whose perspective contradicted His own. In this passage, Jesus shows us the importance of being in agreement with not only God the Father but with those whom we surround ourselves. Jesus knew that if He surrounded Himself with people who spoke against His purpose, He wouldn't be able to accomplish all the Father had sent Him to do. We must be very careful in choosing those we surround ourselves with and whom we allow to influence our emotions, thoughts, and beliefs. (Verse 41) *"Gripping her (firmly) by the hand, He said to her, 'Talitha cumi'—which translated is, 'Little girl, I say to you, arise (from the sleep of death)'.* (Verse 42) *And instantly, the girl got up and started walking around—for she was twelve years old. And they were utterly astonished and overcome with amazement."*

The little girl was twelve years old. A twelve-year-old daughter who died, simultaneously as the woman with the issue of blood, who had been suffering for twelve years, was healed. Both daughters were declared and deemed incurable; however, when they both came in contact with Jesus, they were healed.

Just because the world tells you that you are broken, unworthy, or worthless does not mean you are a lost cause to our Savior. Whether you come boldly and directly to Jesus with your need, like Jairus, or quietly yearning for His help like the woman with the issue, it is important to remind yourself that you are worthy of healing. You are worthy of a new name, a new identity, and a new life. A life that won't allow your issue to define you any longer, for behold, God is doing a new thing!

I was at work one day and came across a giant spider. Spiders freak me out, but I didn't want to kill it, so I found a clear plastic cup and set it on top of the spider and then put a small piece of granite on top of that to ensure the spider would stay in its place while I waited for a co-worker to show up and let it go outside. (I was too scared of the spider to attempt to get it out the door). I kept passing by all day and checking to see if the spider was still there.

As the hours passed, I started to feel bad for the spider; it had no idea what was happening, but I did. I knew that, although it was trapped now, it would eventually be freed. You see, the spider's perspective was entrapment, fear, and being left alone; my perspective was protecting it until the right time came for it to be delivered from its captivity. This got me thinking about life and how many times I felt trapped in my situation, how the panic and anxiety were so overwhelming I couldn't see a way out.

Looking at the helpless spider, I couldn't help but relate to its trapped body, unsure of the future or why the wait was so long. Four hours probably seemed like an eternity to a creature created to be free. With the piece of granite on top, there was no way the spider could move in any direction, only in the small space provided by the cup. In life, we don't always know what God is doing. Sometimes it feels like our situation is closing in on us without any feasible way out. It can feel as though a heavy burden has been placed on us, and all hope of breaking free seems lost. Just like the spider, our wait can seem long, leaving us very much alone. It's in these times that our perspective is extremely crucial. Instead of focusing on the heaviness of the situation, the walls of anxiety and depression closing in on us minute by minute, we have focus on the amazing God outside our draining circumstances.

Just as I was able to lift the granite and free the spider at any time, God, too, has the power, at any moment, to lift your burdens and free you from everything that is weighing you down. Perspective allows us to acknowledge God's timing. It allows us to see from a vantage point that we aren't currently experiencing, and most of all, it builds faith. Faith that there is a way out no matter what our current circumstance is. Our Heavenly Father is already working on and preparing that way. Your situation won't last forever; the burden will lift, and freedom will come at just the right moment and at just the right time.

Some phrases to speak over your life when you need to re-align your perspective:

- The past is behind me; I live fully in the present.
- My prayers are powerful and effective because I am in right standing with God. (Adapted from James 5:16)
- I do not speak idle words, only words that enhance the power of God. (Adapted from Matthew 12:36)

- "Trust in the Lord with all your heart and lean not on your own understanding; in all your ways submit to Him, and He will make your paths straight" – Proverbs 3:5-6 (NIV)
- This is going to end well.
- It is written God is my healer. (Adapted from Psalm 103:3)
- "Even though I walk through the darkest valley, I will fear no evil, for You are with me; Your rod and Your staff, they comfort me." -Psalm 23:4 (NIV)
- God has a permanent solution to my temporary circumstance.
- The Lord goes before me in <u>every</u> scary situation I face.
- I am protected by the Lord on every side; evil can't come near me.
- There is nothing I will face that the Lord and I together can't handle.

# CHAPTER 12: POWER IN YOUR RESPONSE

*"Jesus didn't live in reaction to the devil; he lived in response to the Father."*
--Bill Johnson

Every second of every day, we are given the opportunity to respond with the wisdom of the Holy Spirit or react out of the emotions of the flesh. Whether responding to a family member, a co-worker, or just a thought that randomly pops into our head, we are always given a second to pause and choose how to respond. Responses set the tone for the day, our relationships, and overall mental health.

We often fail to respond with kindness, mercy, and understanding. When we react with our flesh, we tend to be snappy, abrupt, and harsh with our words, acting on the emotion we are feeling at the time, rather than with wisdom and understanding. In life, we want to ensure that our responses model Christ and the promises He made. Throughout Jesus' time here on earth, He was constantly given opportunities to respond. Most of the time, we could easily justify *if* He had responded with the flesh; however, He never did. Jesus consistently set the example of responding with the wisdom of the Holy Spirit.

When Jesus was spending His last night on earth, pleading with His Father to "let this cup pass," the time came for the Roman soldiers to come so Judas could betray Him with a kiss. Jesus knew that the betrayal from Judas, one of his closest friends, would begin the passion leading to his gruesome death.

As previously discussed, Jesus was mentally exhausted and

physically ill during His time in the Garden, begging and pleading with the Father to "let this cup pass" and pleading with His friends to stay up with Him. He must have been so emotionally drained by the time Judas came around with the Roman soldiers.

In Luke 22:47-51, *"And while he was still speaking, behold, there came a crowd, and the man called Judas, one of the Twelve (apostles), was going before them. He drew near Jesus to kiss Him.* (Verse 48) *But Jesus said to him, 'Judas! Would you betray and deliver up the Son of Man with a kiss?'* (Verse 49) *And when those who were around Him saw what was about to happen, they said, 'Lord, shall we strike with the sword?'* (Verse 50) *And one of them struck the bond servant of the high priest and cut off his ear, the right one.* (Verse 51) *But Jesus said, 'Permit them to go so far (as to seize me)' And He touched the little ear and healed him."*

The Gospel of John tells us that Peter was the disciple who cut off the Roman soldier's ear with a sword. Jesus could have easily said, "Yes, Peter, defend me! I have just been betrayed by one of my best friends, and this is so unfair!" He didn't. Jesus had every right to act on emotion during such an exhausting, anxious, and uncertain time, yet He chose peace. Jesus responded with wisdom, knowing that this betrayal needed to happen for the Father's perfect plan to take place. Peter reacted out of fear and anger, immediately pulling out his sword and cutting the ear off of the bondservant. Jesus stops Peter and heals the man who is there to capture Him.

Brothers and sisters, it is vital that even in our most exhausted and anxious state, we respond with wisdom and understanding, knowing that God has a plan greater than the circumstances we face. Our responses will either work with or against our Father in Heaven. Responding with emotion to a temporary circumstance is never in our best interest.

Continuing with Jesus's passion, (Matthew 27:11-17), *"Now Jesus stood before the governor (Pilate), and the governor asked Him, 'Are You the King of the Jews?' Jesus said to him, 'You have stated (the fact).'* (Verse 12) *But when the charges were made against Him by the chief priests and elders, He made no answer.* (Verse 13) *Then Pilate said to Him, 'Do you not hear how many and how serious are the things they are testifying against You?'* (Verse 14) *But He made no reply to him, not even to a single accusation, so that the governor marveled greatly."*

Jesus stayed silent. He was accused of being a terrible person and, yet, stayed silent. How full of wisdom must you be to remain silent when surrounded by horrific lies? In life, we will have moments where the enemy will come at us with full force, covering us with lies about who we are, intending to break us down. Sometimes these lies will come as inaudible thoughts that creep into our heads. Other times they will come from those around us, pointing out our weaknesses and leaving us feeling defeated and unworthy of God's plan for our life.

During my second divorce, my soon to be ex-husband spread horrible lies about me to our church family and friends. I actually ended up losing a very close friend who chose to believe the lies, instead of what she knew my character to be. It was so hurtful, I wanted so badly to defend myself as he made public posts on social media blaming me for leaving him and not keeping my vows before God. I wanted so desperately to set the record straight and clear my name. In the last few months of our marriage, the verbal and emotional abuse had gotten so bad, it started transferring to my daughter. Enough was enough. Living in a home where you were constantly walking on eggshells, woken up getting yelled at, subjected to derogatory comments and escalating outbursts caused so much stress and anxiety. We had to go.

I consulted with three different Christian Counselors before making the decision to leave my second marriage. All three (at separate times) said to leave and never go back. One said that she couldn't help me until I left the toxic environment.

I was so embarrassed and humiliated, having to contemplate this decision only a year after getting married. I cried over letting God down more times than I can count. One divorce, sure, I could justify that. I was very young and found myself pregnant in college. That marriage was me just trying to "do the right thing". This second divorce, I was in my 30's and knew in my heart I had once again married the wrong person because I was so desperate to have a family.

I had once again taken matters into my own hands instead of trusting in and relying on God to send the man He had intended for me (no matter how long that took). I cried over losing my very good friend. I cried over having to sell my home, after only living in it for six months. A home that my daughter and I had waited over a decade to call our own.

As I went through the motions of once again leaving and starting my life over, I thought about Jesus and how He stayed silent while horrific accusations were made against Him. It gave me comfort and peace knowing that as much as I wanted to defend myself, Jesus did too. Then I was reminded that to Jesus, only the Fathers opinion and approval mattered.

During that divorce, I had to remind myself that I am living for an audience of One. As long as I knew I was in constant conversation with the Father and sought His will for my life, it didn't matter what anyone else said.

Jesus never ceases to amaze me, how He chose love and forgiveness over proving his accusers wrong. This was one of the hardest seasons I have walked, constantly feeling judged and shamed for not "fighting" for my marriage and being told that "satan attacks the family first". The judgmental words cut deep. It was easy for those who were only seeing my situation from the outside, to cast and make comments. I was in the throes of severe panic attacks and depression, now dealing with the ramifications of leaving an abusive husband. Meditating on the words of Jesus, all I could do was choose love and forgiveness as well. I couldn't go to everyone on social media and tell my side of the story, that would be impossible and exhausting. I couldn't change the opinions of those who had already made their mind up about me. What I could do was try my best to model Jesus, which was to love, forgive and live for the Father.

So, I am here to say that if you find yourself in this situation, please stay close to the Father, and stay strong. Pray and seek wisdom from qualified, God-centered people, and if you have to, leave. When there is abuse, you leave. I am not an advocate for divorce and even waited three years to sign the papers on my first divorce because I didn't want to give up on the commitment we made before God.

During that period of my life, I had a very wise deacon at my parents' church say, "Sometimes man puts together what God never intended to be together." His words brought me a lot of comfort. You see God doesn't want divorce, but He also doesn't want people who make mistakes to feel obligated to live in torment the rest of their lives. John 10:10 (NIV) says, *"I have come that they may have life, and have it to the full."* Jesus will never turn away a repentant sinner who has made the hard decision to reclaim their life. It took me well over a year to heal from the triggers of my second marriage. I marveled at Jesus as I went through that season of life. I had to remind myself that my Father in heaven knew the truth and that was all that mattered. Silent. Through the accusations, through the judgment, the betrayal, and the embarrassment. Jesus stayed silent. So, if you happen to find yourself in a similar situation, you aren't alone.

Jesus knew all the feelings I was experiencing, yet He didn't respond with emotion to His own trial and tribulations. So, what was His secret? He didn't react to the thoughts and words surrounding Him; instead, He responded with silence, knowing that no response would allow the Father's perfect will for His life to come to pass. Jesus knew that God could do more with His silence than with any words He could have used to defend Himself. Sometimes we need to stay silent. When we try to break the bondage in our lives and inwardly fight with everything we have, the words from those around us can leave us frustrated and angry. We want to shout and defend ourselves, saying, "I am not the same person! You don't know the fight I am fighting to break free from this depression, this anxiety, this addiction!"

But what does shouting do? What do words really do when the accuser has already made up, in their mind, the image of the "you" they want to hold onto? Jesus knew that the chief priests and elders already had their minds made up about who He was and how they wanted everyone else to perceive Him. The scripture says that Pilate couldn't find fault with Jesus, so he sent him to Herod, the ruler of Jesus' jurisdiction. (Luke 23:4-11), *"And Pilate said to the chief priests and the throngs, 'I find no guilt or crime in this Man.'* (Verse 5) *But they were urgent and emphatic, saying, 'He stirs up and excites the people, teaching throughout all Judea-from Galilee, where He began, even to this place.'* (Verse 6) *Upon hearing this, Pilate asked whether the Man was a Galilean.* (Verse 7) *And when he found out that He belonged Herod's jurisdiction, he sent Him up to Herod, who was also in Jerusalem in those days.* (Verse 8) *Now when Herod saw Jesus, he was exceedingly glad, for he had eagerly desired to see Him for a long time because of what he had heard concerning Him, and he was hoping to witness some sign done by Him.* (Verse 9) *So he asked Him many questions, but He made no reply.* (Verse 10) *Meanwhile, the chief priests and the scribes stood by, continuing vehemently and violently to accuse Him.* (Verse 11) *And Herod, with his soldiers, treated Him with contempt and scoffed at and ridiculed Him; then, dressing Him up in bright and gorgeous apparel, he sent Him back to Pilate."*

Silence. In a world where we want to defend ourselves and prove who we are, we must remember that we are in this world but not of it. (John 15:19). Not every attack needs a response. Jesus stayed silent while the Chief Priests and Scribes stood by and violently accused Him. Jesus remained silent while Herod and his soldiers ridiculed Him. Sometimes, a non-response allows the Father to speak louder than our words ever could. When the stone was rolled away, and the tomb was found empty, that spoke louder than anything Jesus could have said to defend the truth of who He was to His accusers. When satan comes at you, bringing up your past, regrets, mistakes, anxieties, addictions, and bondages, stand firm, stand tall, and let the Lord show His glory of who you are in Christ.

Coming to the end of Christ's passion, we come to (Luke 23:32-43), *"Two others also, who were criminals, were led away to be executed with Him.* (Verse 33) *And when they came to the place which is called The Skull [Latin: Calvary; Hebrew: Golgotha], there they crucified Him and the criminals, one on the right and one on the left.* (Verse 34) *And Jesus prayed, 'Father, forgive them, for they know not what they do.' And they divided His garments and distributed them by casting lots for them.* (Verse 35) *Now the people stood by watching; but the rulers scoffed and sneered at Him, saying, 'He rescued others; let Him now rescue Himself, if He is the Christ of God, His Chosen One!'* (Verse 36) *The soldiers also ridiculed and made sport of Him, coming up and offering Him vinegar.* (Verse 37) *And saying, 'If you are the King of the Jews, save Yourself.'* (Verse 38) *For there was also an inscription above Him in letters of Greek and Latin and Hebrew: 'This is the King of the Jews.'* (Verse 39) *One of the criminals who was suspended kept up a railing at Him, saying, 'Are You not the Christ? Rescue Yourself and us!'* (Verse 40) *But the other one reproved him, saying, 'Do you not even fear God, seeing you yourself are under the same sentence of condemnation and suffering the same penalty?* (Verse 41) *And we indeed suffer it justly, receiving the due reward of our actions; but this Man has done nothing out of the way.'* (Verse 42) *Then he said to Jesus, 'Lord, remember me when You come in Your kingly glory!'"* (Verse 43) *And He answered him, 'Truly I tell you, today you will be with Me in Paradise.'"*

So many examples here. So first, Jesus was crucified with two criminals. In His last moments on earth, He was surrounded by people who led lives unlike His own. Jesus' FIRST response was to pray, and in His prayer, He prayed for God the Father to forgive His accusers for what they were doing. I don't know about you, but if I were betrayed by a best friend, spoken horribly about, and sentenced to death, my first response would NOT have been to pray for those mistreating me.

The people then continued to watch, divide up His clothing, the rulers mocked Him, the sign above His head was meant to mock Him, and the criminal next to Him provoked Him, telling Him to essentially prove who He was and save all of them.

The only person to show faith and believe Jesus was Who He said He was, was the second criminal, who asked that Jesus remember him, to which Jesus gave His second response, "Truly I tell you, today you will be with Me in Paradise." Jesus was being tried and tormented at every angle. Yet, His only responses in the last hours of His life were to pray for those against Him and offer deliverance to the criminal who believed in Who He was. How incredible was Jesus' response? Pray, forgive, and deliver.

If only we could learn to respond like Jesus in the face of adversity! To be able to love and forgive when others come against us. To stay silent when the world and our negative thoughts speak against the person we are striving to be, not giving in to the emotions of the flesh but responding with wisdom and truth. Knowing how we respond directly impacts the power we allow God to have in our lives. In a world that teaches us to react on emotion, we must remind ourselves that the response is to the Father, for He alone can turn any mess into a message of survival.

# CHAPTER 13: FAITH > FEAR = SURRENDER

*"Faith and Fear both demand you believe in Something you cannot see. You choose!"* –Bob Proctor

There's a saying that goes, "Your faith seems like a great idea until it's being tested." How many of you have been in the midst of a struggle and had someone come up and say, "You just need to trust God and have more faith." Valid advice, but when every second of your day is spent fighting to survive, that very simple advice is enough to throw you over the edge. Most people have no idea what you are being challenged with, and it's always easier to offer advice outside of someone else's desperate struggle.

So, what do you do when faced with a terrifying circumstance and are given the option to either respond with fear or faith? Romans 12, at the end of verse 3, we are told that God has distributed to each of us a measure of faith. A measure of faith means that God has given each of us enough faith that is required to use the specific gifts He has bestowed on us. That means that if God has set a troubling circumstance before you, and you are doing all you can to live your life to glorify God, then you are also equally equipped with enough faith to walk through the fear of that circumstance.

Satan knows that fear causes us to not trust God. Fear distracts us from our purpose and hinders us from being joyful members of the Body of Christ. If satan can consume our thoughts with fear, then we become very useless when trying to accomplish the plans God has laid out. It is so important to remember that how you choose to respond to your fear determines how much power it will have over you.

Satan thrives on worry and fear. If he can't get you to worry, then he can't defeat you. There are many times, even now, when a negative, scary, or depressing thought will pop into my head. I have to consciously pause, immediately react to the thought, and say/think, "No! I am not going to let this bother me today. I will not let this thought/emotion go on any further than THIS moment because God is in control!" Then, I immediately go back to what I was doing before the thought crept in, and I fight every urge to allow the thought to consume me.

Sometimes I have to stop a few times because the thoughts can be persistent, and that's ok! If the thoughts come at you repeatedly for an hour, you fight them for an hour, and eventually, they will subside. I promise they will subside. Persistence is key in fighting off the attacks of the enemy. We must remember, satan doesn't stand outside with a mega horn and a giant banner; he is sneaky and hides in the shadows. He slips in thoughts every moment he can to trip us up and distract us from doing the will of God.

As we said before, satan's strength is his patience, so our strength needs to be our persistence. If by now you're thinking, "Great… so how am I possibly going to choose faith over fear every single time fear presents itself?" You aren't alone. In fact, Peter faced a situation where he had to choose faith over fear, and fear won for a while. Let's see what Peter did to regain his faith and conquer fear.

Matthew 14:22-33, *"Then He directed the disciples to get into the boat and go before Him to the other side, while He sent away the crowds.* (Verse 23) *And after He had dismissed the multitudes, He went up into the hills by Himself to pray. When it was evening, He was still there alone.* (Verse 24) *But the boat was by this time out on the sea, many furlongs (a furlong is one-eighth of a mile) distant from the land, beaten and tossed by the waves, for the wind was against them.* (Verse 25) *And in the fourth watch (between 3:00 -6:00am) of the night, Jesus came to them, walking on the sea.* (Verse 26) *And when the disciples saw Him walking on the sea, they were terrified and said, 'It is a ghost!' And they screamed out with fright.* (Verse 27) *But instantly He spoke to them, saying, 'Take courage! I AM! Stop being afraid!'* (Verse 28) *And Peter answered Him, 'Lord, if it is You, command me to come to You on the water.'* (Verse 29) *He said, 'Come!' So, Peter got out of the boat and walked on the water, and he came toward Jesus.* (Verse 30) *But when he perceived and felt the strong wind, he was frightened, and as he began to sink, he cried out, 'Lord, save me!'* (Verse 31) *Instantly Jesus reached out His hand and caught and held him, saying to him, 'O you of little faith, why did you doubt?'* (Verse 32) *And when they got into the boat, the wind ceased.* (Verse 33) *And those in the boat knelt and worshipped Him, saying, 'Truly, You are the Son of God!'"*

Let's take a deeper look. If you go back and read the beginning of chapter 14, you will see that Jesus not only cured the sick but also fed the 5,000 with five loaves and two fish. The disciples, including Peter, had just witnessed some of Jesus' incredible miracles. So, it makes you wonder why Peter would have trouble walking to Jesus, even if it was on treacherous water, when he knew firsthand how incredibly powerful Jesus was. This is so comforting to me. Peter knew Jesus personally and still waivered in his faith. In verse 22, Jesus gives a very simple direction to get in the boat and go on ahead of Him.

In life, we will experience many different directions from God. Some will be easy, and some will require intense faith and trust in order to follow through. Peter started with a simple direction, but by the middle of the night, he was given the direction to do the impossible, walk on water. Isn't it funny how we limit God's capabilities? Leaving on a boat, totally easy to obey God. Peter was a fisherman, and his capabilities on the water made him very confident in sailing ahead of the Lord. Walking on water? Not in Peter's wheelhouse. Never in Peter's life had he walked on water, yet the Lord commanded him to.

What I love more than the Lord commanding Peter to walk on water, was the sentence before. Peter questions the Lord, saying, "Lord, if it is You, command me to come to You on the water." How many times in life do we question the Lord? "Is this relationship right for me?" "Should I take the job across the country?" "Lord, if you are all powerful, can't you take this anxiety away? Take this depression away? Lord, can't you take this addiction away if You really are who You say You are?"

We have all been a Peter. I certainly have. What we have to remember is that when we are questioning the Lord, He almost always responds with a command. Our breakthroughs never come without taking the first step of faith.

During the height of my depression, anxiety, and panic attacks, I can still picture myself now in my kitchen, shaking as I was making breakfast and telling God, "Use me. Use this awful, terrible, and scary experience to help others. Whatever I have to go through in order for you to use me, I'm ok with." In all honestly, I was terrified. I wanted the panic to stop. I wanted the shaking, the hyperventilating, and the uncontrollable moments of anxiety and depression to stop. I continually prayed that my anxiety pills would kick in faster so I could get some relief. I wanted everything to stop. But I knew my God, and I knew He could take whatever mess I was in and turn it into Something beautiful to help others who were also struggling. I knew that if God promised to make beauty from ashes, and there were others before me who had been restored through God, then I, too, could be restored. My faith in God had to overcome my fear of the current situation I was facing.

Brothers and sisters, there will be times when God puts a command on our hearts that we don't see as humanly impossible. We put God in a box, and if we can't fathom how the direction will come to fruition, we tend to disregard the direction. How could God ask us to do Something we can't see the outcome of? Faith. We must walk by faith, which means that we acknowledge the power of God and walk in His authority, believing what He says to be true, even if we cannot see it yet.

When we walk in fear, we choose to walk in our own emotions, which can misinterpret the truth that God is speaking in our life. Walking in fear is when we only focus on what we see in the moment. When we cloud our vision with emotion, it's nearly impossible to see the deliverance God has in store. In Verse 30, Peter was walking confidently in faith, and as soon as he felt a strong wind, he became afraid, started to sink, and shouted out for the Lord to save him.

I've been there. Taking the brave first step of faith and then having the whispers of satan bombard my mind causing me to lose sight of the Lord. I start to shake, to panic, to hyperventilate. I shift my focus from God and begin to sink. I sink back into depression. I sink back into anxiety; I sink back into the addiction of needing control. My life spirals, my job starts to fail, my finances begin to fail, my relationships start to fail, and I cry out against the strong wind that's whipping hard against me with the very little voice I have left, just like Peter did, "Lord, save me!". "Lord, save me from every attack that is coming against me. Save me from my doubt in You. Lord, save me from myself."

You see, our faith needs to roar louder than the wind of doubt coming against us. It needs to stand in truth and not by the emotion we are experiencing. In Ireland, when someone is consumed with an emotion, instead of saying, I am afraid they would say, "The spirit of fear is upon me." When we change our wording, we change the power our words have over our life. Instead of claiming fear as part of their identity, they claim that the fear is only visiting, and is not attached to who they are as a person.

I think this is both beautiful and important. When we are presented with the struggle of panic, addiction, depression, and anxiety, we need to change our wording. We need to stop saying, "I'm anxious, I'm depressed, I'm panicking, I'm addicted." Change the narrative. Those things are not who you are. Go back to Chapter 1. Who are you? You are made in the image and likeness of God. Anxiety, depression, addiction, panic—they are just visiting. They aren't here to stay because nowhere in the Bible does it say God made you to suffer that way for the rest of your life.

Actually, quite the contrary. In the Bible, Jesus specifically tells us in John 14:27 that He leaves us His peace, which is quite the opposite of fear. Just like anything in life, when something visits, it means that it also leaves. Faith assures us that God is bigger, stronger, and more powerful than any visiting struggle; faith also requires us to believe that this is true. In order to walk by faith, we need to know the heart of God. We need to know His character so we can believe His words.

Peter knew the character of the Lord, and when he started to sink and cried out for help, the Bible says that Jesus *instantly* reached out His hand, caught him, held him, and asked him why he had such little faith. Instantly. When we cry out to Jesus, He *instantly* reaches back for us. We may not feel His touch at that exact moment, but our faith can give us confidence that when we are in trouble, Jesus is never far away.

It was October of 2021, and I was a solid four months in, waking up multiple times a night, each time in a cold sweat, heart-racing panic. Every. Single. Night. I found myself pacing, praying, and pleading with the Lord in the early morning hours for my panic attacks to be taken away. Night after night, I would wake up, and night after night, I would pace and shake and cry and beg and eventually fall asleep, just to be awakened… again… and again. Those four months were mentally, emotionally, physically, and spiritually draining. I was working a full-time job when my daughter was in school. She was struggling because I was struggling as I battled my panic attacks, anxiety, and depression. My second husband and I were purchasing our first home, and he was barely working and helping to contribute to our family's needs (financially, emotionally, physically, and spiritually) which put an even greater strain on me.

The pressure was on. By the end of my day, I was exhausted, drained, and in need of sleep, sleep that I wasn't able to get. Rest seemed to elude me over those four months, which took a heavy toll on me. I gained excessive weight, struggled to be present at my job, and, more importantly, struggled to be the mom I needed to be at home. The panic during the day took on a whole new level at night, and I couldn't escape the reality I was experiencing.

So, this is where God is good. A few weeks before my constant panic started, my church happened to be selling tickets for a women's retreat in October hosted by Pastors Sean and Christa Smith. I immediately signed up and got my mom a ticket as well. Little did I know that attending that conference would change my life. It is important to remember that no matter what, God is all-knowing, loving, and always providing for His children. He put it on my heart to purchase the tickets and to get my mother one as well (little did she know that she would end up chauffeuring a very panicked, tired, and emotionally drained daughter around that weekend). God also knew what to put on Sean and Christa's hearts as they spoke that weekend, but we will get to that part a little later. You need to always remember that God prepares a way; when we see no way, when we don't know we need a way, He is always one step ahead.

OK, so fast forward. We were supposed to settle on a house in August before school started, but at the last minute, it fell through. We found another house that we ended up settling on October 8$^{TH}$. The conference was on October 15$^{th}$. By this time, I had had my fair share of emotional breakdowns. It is now the first night of the conference, and as we close in prayer, Pastor Sean is praying over everyone. He specifically says, "There is someone here who needs rest, they need sleep, Lord, and I know you are going to give it to them." Well, that was about all I needed to hear before I jumped up for that altar call. I squeezed my way up to the front and was convinced that the words he was saying were for me. They had to be for me! Who else in that room was experiencing the panic I was experiencing multiple times a night?

Surely, I was the special attendee picked out for God's blessing.

My mom and I went home, and as I tucked myself in bed, I thanked God for the good night's sleep I was about to get and fell asleep…for about two hours, and then I woke up. Panicked. Shaking. Sweating and back to pacing around pleading with the Lord. I finally fall back asleep, and two hours later, repeat. I woke up at one am, three am, and five am that night, no different than any other night. No different because the promise that Pastor Sean spoke over the women at the conference clearly wasn't for me. I was defeated. By the time I woke up at five am, I just sat and cried. I was exhausted, angry, hurt, and felt absolutely forgotten by God.

By the time six am rolled around, my mom asked how I slept and if I was ready to head out for the second half of the conference. I just looked at her and started crying. I did NOT want to go back to the conference because why would I? God clearly didn't care about me. Then Something in me just stopped, and I looked at my mom and said, "Yes. I am exhausted, and I didn't sleep, and God didn't help me, but it's always the times when you don't want to go that God wants you there the most, so we're going". Let's say I was shaking the entire time, like trembling with anxiety running all through my body. I was so uncomfortable that when the lunch intermission hit, I jumped out of my seat and bee-lined it straight for Pastor Christa. My mom, for a quick second, said, "What are you doing?" To which I quickly responded, "I'm going to have her pray directly over me so there isn't a chance that God doesn't know who the blessing is for." I wasn't giving up without a fight. If the blessing wasn't coming to me, then I was going to find it.

Remember Marvina, my Prayer Warrior that I thanked at the beginning of the book? Guess who was sitting right next to Christa? See, God is good and always one step ahead. Marvina caught my eye, saw me heading that way, and introduced me to Christa. I stood before her and could barely get the words out, "Please pray for me." She asked what was wrong, and I just sobbed. (Now, keep in mind, I am not by any stretch of the mind a crier. It takes a lot for me to cry, especially in public and especially in front of a woman I had never met.)

Christa prayed with me for a while, and the whole time she spoke, I begged God. The prayer ended, and we headed outside for lunch. I wasn't feeling much different, but I figured miracles take time, right? We head back in for the last portion of the conference. Christa spoke about Hannah in the Bible, and like previously mentioned in the book, how she felt that God had forgotten her. My ears perked up. That was me; I felt forgotten. I hung onto to every word Christa spoke and kept telling myself that if God can remember Hannah, I need to have faith that He would remember me, too. We started singing a worship song, and as I stood and stared at the cross on the altar, I begged and pleaded with God, "Please, God, please. Please take this away. Please help me sleep. Please remember me like you remembered Hannah." The song continued, and as my begging tapered off, my mind went silent, and I decided to go a different route with God.

How many of you have used reverse psychology to get what you want, or at least attempt to get what you want? Brothers and sisters, that's the level of desperation I was at. Yup. I decided mid-worship song to try reverse psychology on God. I immediately went to, *OK, fine. Don't heal me, don't help me. I didn't really need Your help. I just thought that since You were in the business of helping people, You might want to help me too, but it's cool. I don't need it.* How desperate we can get when begging and pleading with God!?

This went on for a few minutes until I transitioned one more time in my silent conversation with God. Begging wasn't working; reverse psychology, although creative, wasn't going to get me the freedom I was so desperately searching for. I just stared at the cross, closed my eyes, and told God in my heart. *Look, I really, really, really want You to heal me. I want to feel normal again. I want to enjoy life again. I want to feel freedom from this anxiety that is gripping me every second of my day. But I love You, and nothing will ever change that. We have been through so much together, and You have always been there, so if You don't take this anxiety away, and if You don't free me from this panic, I'll be ok. I won't be happy about it, I won't understand it, but I promise You, no matter what You do or don't do, I will never love You any less.*

I surrendered. People always talk about surrendering to the Lord, and I never knew what that meant until that day. Surrendering means setting aside every desire of your heart because you love God more.

That day, I made up my mind that no matter what God allowed in my life, I would never love Him any less, and that opened my heart, mind, and soul to the blessing I received just a few minutes later. You see, by this time, the song had ended, and Pastor Sean was saying the final prayer of the conference. He was listing specific ailments to pray over everyone. Right toward the end of his prayer, he said, "I also want to pray for someone here who is struggling with Hypoglycemia (low blood sugar) and severe panic attacks."

I started to tear up. I closed my eyes and said, "God, please. I will never love You any less, but please help me." My eyes were closed, and I felt this sensation come over my entire head. It was a magnetic sensation that lasted just a few seconds and honestly freaked me out a little. I looked at my mom and said, "Something just happened. I felt something in my head." We walked to the car, and as we got home and prepared for bed that night, I didn't have high hopes for a good night's sleep. However, I had faith enough to believe that with God, certainly, all things were still possible. The truth was, even if I did wake up and panic every night, I knew He would at least be near me. I fell asleep and woke up…EIGHT HOURS LATER.

I slept. The next night, I slept, and the next night and the next night. A year passed, and although my daytime panic attacks lingered for a few more months while I navigated a less toxic living arrangement, I could sleep. I thank God for Pastor Sean and Pastor Christa. I thank God for Cornerstone Church and for all the wonderful pastors there. Having faith to face and overcome your fears isn't easy. It certainly isn't easy to surrender to a life of struggle because you love God; however, God is faithful. He is good, and He will restore the brokenness you carry as long as you fully surrender to Him and His will.

# CHAPTER 14: PEACE

*"Peace begins with a smile."* –Mother Teresa

*"Peace, I leave with you; my peace I give you. I do not give to you as the world gives. Do not let your hearts be troubled and do not be afraid."* (John 14:27 NIV). Peace is something we are given freely yet struggle daily to find. How can one find peace in the middle of panic? When chaos surrounds you during the most anxious moments of your life, where do you find the peace you were originally given? Chris Gore says, "Peace is not the absence of something; it's the presence of someone—Jesus!"

A lot of times in life, we feel like we have to eliminate things in order to have peace. Less clothes, lighter workload, fewer appointments on the calendar. We work so hard to eliminate things, thinking that we will magically find peace. The answer isn't removing anything but rather adding the presence of God into everything we do. Jesus didn't say, "My peace, I leave you when you forget all about Me and decide to handle life on your own." That would be ridiculous. He gave us His peace with the expectation that we would do life *with* Him, even after His time on earth was over.

If we are struggling to find His peace, we may need to look at what we're adding to our lives, and if it isn't Him, then we should start there. Let's take a look at Martha and Mary in the Bible. Luke 10: 38-42, *"Now while they were on their way, it occurred that Jesus entered a certain village, and a woman named Martha received and welcomed Him into her house.* (Verse 39) *And she had a sister named Mary, who seated herself at the Lord's feet and was listening to His teaching.* (Verse 40) *But Martha was distracted with much serving; and she came up to Him and said, 'Lord, is it nothing to You that my sister has left me to serve alone? Tell her then to help me!'* (Verse 41) *But the Lord replied to her by saying, 'Martha, Martha, you are anxious and troubled about many things.* (Verse 42) *There is need of only one or but a few things. Mary has chosen the good portion, which shall not be taken away from her.'"*

Martha and Mary were sisters, living in the same house Jesus had been invited to enter. Mary recognized Who Jesus was and chose to sit at His feet and listen to His words. Martha allowed herself to be consumed with the anxiety and worries of hosting such a special guest that she missed out on the personal experience He was offering. What is the difference between Martha and Mary? Mary chose to let the chaos around her go while she internally rested in the peace of Christ. In contrast, Martha consumed her evening with external stress and confusion, not adding Christ into the equation. Takeaway, be a Mary.

I love that Martha went to Jesus and had the audacity to complain that her sister wasn't helping. How many times do we go to God complaining about our circumstances, only to realize that the circumstances would be different if we allowed ourselves to rest in the presence of God? God is powerful, and God is peace; therefore, where your peace is, there too is where your power lies.

We can learn from Martha and Mary that peace is a choice, and our happiness is indirectly tied to peace. When we allow our lives to be affected in every way by our Lord and Savior, His peace will flow in us and around us. (NLT, Isaiah 26:3), *"You will keep in perfect peace all who trust in You, all whose thoughts are fixed on You."* When we trust in God, we eliminate fear. We know He has our back and will help us handle anything that comes our way." (NIV, John 16:33) *"I have told you these things, so that in Me you may have peace. In this world you will have trouble. But take heart! I have overcome the world."*

Jesus doesn't eliminate peace; He offers a safe haven amid chaos for all who trust and believe in Him. We are promised that in the world, we will have trouble. Anxiety, panic, addiction, and depression will rear their ugly heads at us relentlessly. Until we are in Heaven, we will never be free from the troubles of the world; however, if we rest in the hope of Jesus and His word, we can have the peace of knowing that in the end, He wins. With it, our eternal life of peace comes.

The peace of Christ comes when we know God is in control and His mind is set on us. So, what are some things we can do to enhance the peace of Christ in our lives? First, we can stop taking offense. Taking offense causes strife and, in turn, anxiety. (ESV, James 1:19), *"Know this, my beloved brothers; let every person be quick to hear, slow to speak; slow to anger."* We are not called to react to everything that bothers us. Filter with the Holy Spirit and let it go. The more tension and strife you hold onto, the less room you have to rest in the peace of Christ. When we hold onto grudges and resentment, we do more harm to ourselves than it's worth.

Having healthy boundaries from toxic people is absolutely OK; however, we must remember to set the boundary, let go of the hurt and let God handle the rest. We tend to get caught up in complaining, gossiping, and harping on the person or circumstance that did us wrong. That just keeps us in captivity and bondage longer, again taking up room where the peace of Christ should be.

Peace is a choice and should be practiced constantly. Every day we are given the opportunity of peace or chaos by our decisions. When we choose to respond with the love of Christ over hate, judgment, or irritability, we win. We eliminate extra unwanted emotions that would otherwise pile up and consume the home where peace should reside.

Lastly, we need to speak life into dead situations. It is easy to lose sight of peace when the walls crumble around us. Speaking God's truth into a seemingly dead situation will plant hope, opening the door to peace. So, when you are faced with a trial and feel as though peace is a million miles away, look at ways you can add Christ into your life, routine, and chaotic existence, then watch how He will transform you from the inside out. Be a Mary. Choose to sit at the feet of Jesus despite all the chaos around you, and you will receive serenity and peace simply by being with Him.

# CHAPTER 15: JOY

*"Joy does not simply happen to us. We have to choose joy and keep choosing it every day. It is a choice based on the knowledge that we belong to God and have found in God our refuge and our safety and that nothing, not even death, can take God away from us."* –Henri Nouwen

I'm going to level with you. This chapter was terrible to write. You wouldn't believe how many "un-joyful" things happened while writing this chapter. I actually texted Dan, my counselor, about an issue that came up and then joked, "I'm going to start writing my chapter on joy now... lol". I say this half-jokingly and entirely seriously. The devil does NOT want you to be joyful. His main goal is to steal your joy and make you miserable. No one wants to be around a miserable Christian. If you are miserable, then you won't have an impact on those around you. Well, you won't have a POSITIVE impact on those around you. How many miserable Christians have you met and thought, "Good grief, I don't know if I want to be like them!"

You're right. We DON'T want to be like them. We want to be joyful Christians who radiate the goodness of Christ in everything we do. So how do we accomplish being joyful Christians when dealing with not-so-joyful circumstances? Honestly, that question held this book up for almost two months.

What is joy? Certainly, I wasn't feeling it, but the Bible says we have it, so what is it? Joy is happiness that is dependent on who Jesus is and not who we are or what circumstances surround us on any given day.

Psalm 126:3 (NIV) says, *"The Lord has done great things for us, and we are filled with joy."* No matter what we face in life, the fact that God sent His only Son to die for us so that if we believe in Him and live according to His will we can enjoy eternal life in Heaven, is certainly reason enough to choose pure joy! Romans 15:13 (NIV) states, *"May the God of hope fill you with all joy and peace as you trust in Him, so that you may overflow with hope by the power of the Holy Spirit."*

God gave us hope in the form of His Son, Jesus, so that no matter how desperate, anxious, depressed, or damaged we may feel, we can find joy and peace when we choose to trust God and hand over our unfavorable circumstances to Him. By putting our problems in God's hands, we allow Him to take control while we rest in the joy of who He is and the peace that He surrounds us with.

Trusting God is not always easy; however, handing our problems over to Him allows our focus to be transferred from our anxiety, panic, depression, and addiction to a new focus of praising God and celebrating who He is and what He has done and will do for us.

*"The Lord is my strength and my shield; my heart trusts in Him, and He helps me. My heart leaps for joy, and with my song I praise Him."* (NIV, Psalm 28:7). When we hand our problems over to the Lord, He becomes our shelter. He covers us with love and helps us through all adversity. When we praise the Lord, we replace negative emotions with joy, which assures us that God has everything under control. The Christian band Rend Collective has a song, "Joy of the Lord," the lyrics of which give an excellent example of overcoming our earthly troubles by praising God.

The joy of the Lord is your strength when you focus on how wonderful God is and not how terrible your circumstances are. When our focus is on God, His focus is on our problem. Read that again. *When our focus is on God, His focus is on our problem.*

The woman at the well is another one of my favorite women in the Bible, partially because I relate to her humiliation of being married multiple times and partially because Jesus chose this outcast of a woman, in the heat of the day, at the well, to encounter the Savior of the world. John 4:3-7, *"He left Judea and returned to Galilee. It was necessary for Him to go through Samaria. And in doing so, He arrived at a Samaritan town called Sychar, near the tract of land that Jacob gave to his son Joseph. And Jacob's Well was there. So, Jesus, tired as He was from His journey, sat down to rest by the well. It was then about the sixth hour (about noon). Presently, when a woman of Samaria came along to draw water, Jesus said to her, 'Give me a drink.'"* Jesus, a Jew, had to journey through Samaria to meet this particular woman. An important takeaway here, it was about noon, the heat of the day. The women of the town journeyed to get water from the well in the early morning hours to avoid the heat. The woman at the well was an outcast and looked down upon by the other women because of her multiple husbands, so she made the journey alone in the middle of the day to avoid judgment.

Sound familiar? How many times in life have we inconvenienced ourselves in order to avoid shame and judgment from others? I can't tell you how many times I kept myself in unfavorable circumstances purely based on the embarrassment of a mistake. I love that Jesus meets this woman exactly where she is, in an unfavorable and embarrassing circumstance. I love even more that Jesus took the long and unfavorable route to find her.

You see, Jesus also inconvenienced Himself, bringing judgment to His actions for being around Samarian people as a Jewish man. Jesus chose inconvenience because His love for the embarrassed, broken, and outcast woman at the well was greater. (Verse 9) *"The Samaritan woman said to Him, 'How is it that You, being a Jew, ask me, a Samaritan woman for a drink? For the Jews have nothing to do with the Samaritans.'* (Verse 10) *Jesus answered her, 'If you had only known and had recognized God's gift and Who this is that is saying to you, 'Give me a drink,' you would have asked Him (instead) and He would have given you living water.'* (Verse 11) *She said to Him, 'Sir, You have nothing to draw with (no drawing bucket), and the well is deep; how then can you provide living water?* (Verse 12) *Are you greater than and superior to our ancestor Jacob, who gave us this well and who used to drink from it himself, and his sons and his cattle also?'* (Verse 13) *Jesus answered her, 'All who drink of this water will be thirsty again.* (Verse 14) *But whoever takes a drink of the water I will give him shall never, no never be thirsty anymore. But the water that I will give him shall become a spring of water welling up within him unto eternal life.'* (Verse 15) *The woman said to Him, 'Sir, give me this water, so that I may never get thirsty nor have to come here to draw.'* (Verse 16) *At this, Jesus said to her, 'Go, call your husband and come back here.'* (Verse 17) *The woman answered, 'I have no husband.' Jesus said to her, 'You have spoken truly in saying, I have no husband.* (Verse 18) *For you have had five husbands and the man you are now living with is not your husband. In this you have spoken truly.'* (Verse 19) *The woman said to Him, 'Sir, I see and understand that you are a prophet.'"*

So, let's recap, the woman at the well does her best to avoid everyone to the point that she chooses to draw water from the well in the heat of the day. She then runs into a Jewish man (Jesus) and reminds Him that Jews don't like Samarians. He then offers her living water if she will only go and get her husband. This is a complete setup because Jesus knows that she hasn't had just one husband but several.

The woman who tried so hard to avoid her unfavorable past is now face to face with Jesus, Who speaks the truth about her life, a life that she has so desperately tried to hide from everyone else. (Verse 25) *"The woman said to Him, 'I know that Messiah is coming. He who is called the Christ; and when He arrives, He will tell us everything we need to know and make it clear to us.'* (Verse 26) *Jesus said to her, 'I Who now speak with you am He.'* (Verse 27) *Just then, His disciples came, and they wondered (were surprised and astonished) to find Him talking with a woman. However, not one of them asked Him, 'What are You inquiring about?' or 'What do you want?' or 'Why do you speak with her?'* (Verse 28) *Then the woman left her water jar and went away to the town. And she began telling the people,* (Verse 29) *'Come, see a Man who has told me everything that I ever did! Can this be the Christ?'* (Verse 30) *So the people left the town and set out to go to Him."*

Brothers and sisters, sometimes our greatest joy comes in confessing our weakness to the One who loves us most. Jesus HAD to go through Samaria in the middle of the day in order to meet the woman at the well. I'm sure there were more "qualified, holy, and righteous" women He could have met in the morning, but He chose her. I don't think its coincidence that Jesus chose the woman who had the heaviest burden to spread the news of His arrival.

When the Savior meets you exactly where you are, in unfavorable circumstances, the only thing you can feel is joy. Joy that He chose you to share His good news with others. The woman at the well was so excited. The Bible says she left her drawing bucket and ran to town, excited that Jesus saw her for who she really was, yet He still offered her living water.

If you have made mistakes and felt so lost with depression, anxiety, panic, and addiction that you couldn't imagine how anyone could love you, I want you to think really hard about the woman at the well. How Jesus acknowledged her past and still used her to expand His kingdom. In fact, Jesus' conversation with the woman at the well is the longest recorded conversation between Jesus and anyone in the Gospel of John.

You are not worthless because of a mistake or even multiple mistakes. It's so easy to get wrapped up in failure that we miss out on the joy of being loved by God. Don't let your past steal the happiness Jesus died for you to have. James 1: 2-3 says it so beautifully, *"Consider it wholly joyful, my brethren, whenever you are enveloped in or encounter trials of any sort or fall into various temptations. Be assured and understand that the trial and proving of your faith bring out endurance and steadfastness and patience."*

Consider trials and temptations *wholly* joyful. Wow, that basically goes against every ounce of natural human emotion. James is telling us that our faith will bring out endurance, steadfastness, and patience, which will bring us joy because we are growing closer to God. We are not obligated to entertain every emotion that is presented to us. Joy is a choice that no matter what comes our way, we can rest assured that God is working the trial/ struggle out for our good. Nothing but a closer and more intimate relationship with our Savior can come from it.

I was visiting a local church one Sunday and took a random seat right in front of a special needs man named Bill. I'm not going to lie; I went into the service hoping to get some inspiration on this chapter of joy that I had been struggling so hard to write. As I sat through the entirety of the service, Bill kept speaking and praying loudly—very loudly—behind me. At first, I was annoyed and was trying to focus on what the pastor was saying. Then, halfway through the sermon, I realized that God wanted me to hear what Bill was saying more.

You see, Bill kept repeating over and over, "I didn't deserve it. I didn't deserve the divorce, I didn't deserve my medical problems, I didn't deserve my wife leaving me, I didn't deserve my father having a stroke, I didn't deserve it." Loudly, Bill kept repeating this sentence during the sermon, during the songs, and even during the offering. I heard it so many times that tuning it out wasn't an option anymore. I finally sat there with my Bible open, listening to Bill's words drown out the pastor, when it hit me…

Like Bill, I had many things happen to me in life that I felt I didn't deserve. A husband who left me to raise a daughter essentially on my own. I bounced from home to home for years with my daughter while my first husband kept the same address and a comfortable place to live. A second husband who was verbally, mentally and emotionally abusive to both my daughter and me. It got so bad that we had to pack up and leave our home while he was at work one day. All I wanted my whole life was a husband and a family, yet somehow that always eluded me.

As I heard Bill's words, I couldn't help but relate to his pain. I didn't deserve it either. But then I started thinking about my chapter on joy, and it clicked. In John 16:33 (NIV), we hear the wonderful words of our Savior, *"I have told you these things, so that in Me you may have peace. In this world you will have trouble. But take heart! I have overcome the world."*

Jesus never promised that our life would be free from situations and circumstances that were a struggle to get through. He promised actually that we WOULD have trouble. Just like we don't deserve the pain we have suffered, the panic, the anxiety, the addiction that consumes us, we also don't deserve the joy that Jesus offers freely either. You see, maybe joy is happiness we don't deserve, while satan is busy slamming us with pain and suffering we don't deserve.

The joy of the Lord is really a gift from God to combat the sorrow satan tries to throw on our lives. The closer we get to God, the more His joy will flow into our spirit and cover the unjust sorrow and trials of the world. So instead of focusing on everything terrible that we don't deserve, let's change our verbiage and start to say, "Lord, you have done so much for me, and I am filled with joy over the love you have for me. My panic may be rising, my depression deepening, and my addiction consuming. Still, You are the keeper of my heart and the only one who has the power to bring beauty from ashes (Isaiah 61:3) and give me more than I deserve, not because of who I am, but because of Who You are, and that is enough to turn any trial into joy." Joy gives you a choice to view your trial as an opportunity to grow closer to God.

# CHAPTER 16: PROMISES

*"God's promises are always a perfect match for our problems."*
–Lysa TerKeurst

The Bible is flooded with promises from God. In fact, in an article written by Victor Knowles, he references a man, Everett R. Storms, who, after reading the Bible twenty-seven times, concluded that there were 8,810 promises, 7,487 of those promises being made from God to mankind. That's a LOT of promises! So how do we know that those promises are for us? What if we aren't deserving enough, good enough, or holy enough to reap the rewards of such promises?

Throughout the Bible, the word "whosoever" is used repeatedly. I want you to remember as you read this chapter that the promises of God are for "Whosoever will." The word "Whosoever" includes every single one of us. How comforting that the promises of God aren't for a select and elite group, but for whosoever will believe in Jesus as their Lord.

So, what do some of these promises look like? (NIV, Isaiah 41:10), *"So, do not fear, for I am with you; do not be dismayed, for I am your God. I will strengthen you and help you; I will uphold you with My righteous right hand."* God promises to strengthen you when you are weak. An everlasting help when we are afraid and discouraged. (NIV, Matthew 5:4), *"Blessed are those who mourn, for they will be comforted."* When we are grieving and feeling the deepest sadness that we have ever felt, God promises to comfort us. (ESV, Psalm 34:17) says, *"When the righteous cry for help, the*

*Lord hears and delivers them out of all their troubles."* God promises to always listen and always be attentive as we cry out to Him for help, delivering us from our deepest fears.

(ESV, Psalm 46:1), *"God is our refuge and strength; a very present help in trouble."* God promises to be our helper whenever we face a situation or circumstance that we do not know how to handle or feel like we cannot bear alone. God is there to be a very present help whenever we need Him.

(NIV, Matthew 11:28), *"Come to Me, all you who are weary and burdened, and I will give you rest."* God promises to give us rest when we are too tired to go one more step. When life overwhelms us to the point of collapsing, God is there to cover you in a blanket of rest.

(NIV, 2 Corinthians 9:8), *"And God is able to bless you abundantly, so that in all things at all times, having all you need, you will abound in every good work."* God promises to meet every need you have.

(NIV, Isaiah 54:17), *"No weapon forged against you will prevail, and you will refute any tongue that accuses you. This is the heritage of the servants of the Lord, and this is their vindication from me, declares the Lord."* God promises to protect you from the attacks of the enemy.

(NIV, John 8:36), *"So if the Son sets you free, you will be free indeed."* God promises that whoever goes to His Son Jesus, believing in who He is, will be set free.

(NIV, 1 John 1:9), *"If we confess our sins, He is faithful and just and will forgive us our sins and purify us from all unrighteousness."* God promises to forgive all sins we present to Him, giving freely the forgiveness and purification to wipe the slate clean and try again.

(NIV, Isaiah 44:22), *"I have swept away your offenses like a cloud, your sins like the morning mist. Return to me, for I have redeemed you."* God promises to redeem us and never leave us in the mess we have created as long as we repent and return to Him and His will for our lives.

(NIV, Isaiah 26:3), *"You will keep in perfect peace those whose minds are steadfast because they trust in You."* God promises to keep you in perfect peace if you keep Him steadfastly at the center of your life, focusing and filtering your life solely through Him and His word, being unwavering in your focus so as to not let the enemy distract you and bring you down.

God's promises are something we need to not just read but rely on entirely and wholly, never forgetting that the Bible is the LIVING word of God. If those promises exist, they are living promises that will never run out. I encourage you to open your Bible and take the time to locate the promises of God, write them down, meditate on them, and speak them over your life as you continue your journey of hope and healing. When the enemy starts to feed your mind with doubt, claiming that the promises of God are not for you, I want you to stand your ground and declare: "I am a whosoever! And I believe that the promises of God chase me down and surround me with every step, every decision, and every word I speak. There is NOWHERE I can go that the Promises of God won't find me!"

# CHAPTER 17: TESTIMONY OF TRIUMPH

*"Do not pray for an easy life; pray for the strength to endure a difficult one."*
–Bruce Lee

Webster's Dictionary defines "Testimony" as 1) a solemn declaration, 2) Evidence, and 3) An outward sign. It has been said that in order to have a testimony, one must first pass a test. In case you haven't figured it out, the test is life. What you choose to believe in and how you choose to respond when life surprises you with unexpected challenges will help mold you and grow you into the person Christ intended you to be.

Tests in life can strip you of everything that makes you feel comfortable, safe, and secure. These tests will cut away all of your fleshly imperfections, wants, and desires and leave you vulnerable and open so that only God can fill the spaces, completing you in ways you never thought possible. Sometimes we are left feeling so shaken and broken that the only way to overcome is by relying entirely on God and trusting He will see us through.

What's incredible is that each and every one of us is given a path to walk and a unique testimony to give. #1, "A solemn declaration": Proclaim over your life that the fears that consumed you, the addictions that controlled you, and the depression that drained you are no match for the power of the living God in your life. #2, The "evidence" of a changed life will overflow in everything you do. You will start to speak differently, carry yourself differently, and, most importantly, think differently. The controlling thoughts and desires will still come at you, but you will be prepared to shut down the attacks from the enemy at the slightest onset. This does not mean that panic attacks, addictions, and anxiety will be gone forever; it means that we are fully equipped with the word of God to handle every attack that comes our way with minimal disruption to our daily lives. We are able to recognize the trigger, speak life back to the trigger and move on without letting it consume us and drag us down.

Lastly, #3 is the "outward sign." The transformation from who you were to who you are will be visible to everyone who comes in contact with you. In the TV series "The Chosen," Mary Magdalene is confronted by the High Priest Nicodemus, who sees her in the market, healed, and calls her by the name Lilith (her prostitute name in the show). Mary tells Nicodemus that she doesn't go by that name anymore, that her name is Mary (the name given to her at birth), and the name Jesus called her when He healed her. Nicodemus begs Mary to tell him who healed her. Mary doesn't know Jesus' name at this point, so her answer is simply, "I was one way…and now I am completely different. And the thing that happened in between was Him."

He is the only one Who will call us by our birth names when the whispers of satan and the world around us call us by our anxiety, our depression, and our addiction. God *never* loses sight of who we are. To have a testimony of triumph, we must remind ourselves of our desperate past and how far we have come with the help of God.

Your story will unlock the prison someone else is trapped in. The unique experience you have walked through is not in vain; it's not without purpose. God has a plan for your life that is different than the plan for anyone else's. Different. You must come to the realization that your path, your life, and your daily routine will not look like those around you.

For years I tried to mimic others' eating habits, gym routines, praying habits, and parenting strategies. Hell, I even dressed like Brie VanDeCamp for an entire year because she portrayed a woman who "had it all together" in the TV show "Desperate Housewives." Spoiler alert: it didn't work.

I sit back and laugh at myself now, thinking about the absurd things I would do in order to feel normal. What I came to realize is that I am not them, and they are not me. There is no "normal," and accepting that is truly liberating. For instance, my body functions better if I eat small meals throughout the day. That doesn't mean something is wrong with me because I can't do a fasting diet without feeling absolutely awful.

Waking up and going to the gym in the morning is awesome if you are one of those people that can do that and function for the rest of the day. Personally, I enjoy working out at the end of my day when I feel like I have enough of a reserve to sustain a strenuous exercise. Working out on an almost empty stomach freaks me out, and it's just not something I enjoy.

We need to let go of the "mold" of normal and perfect. For years I felt like I was failing because I did things differently than those around me. Then I realized that doing things differently is exactly what makes me uniquely created by God for a purpose only He understands. One thing I am sure of is that God did not want a bunch of robots running around. He wants real people with real fears and struggles who need Him desperately and rely on Him completely. There is a saying that goes, "What's normal to the spider is chaos for the fly."

People may not understand your quirks, but those quirks are precisely what allows the awesomeness of God to flow through you. After all of the years I spent praying to be "normal" and stressing to mold myself like everyone else around me, I can finally say that I am grateful for every imperfection and flaw that I used to desperately plead with God to change. Our testimonies come from a very imperfect life affected by a very perfect God.

You see, you will never be the person you follow on Instagram, the neighbor you admire, or the relative that seems practically perfect in every way. In fact, I can almost guarantee that you will be a mess for at least 50% of your life (and that's being generous). Those people who you strive to be like, you need to understand that they are also a mess, too.

The difference is our perspective. We see what we want to see and overlook others' imperfections. We see in other people what we lack and then get jealous of their lives. We need to look to God for what we lack and trust that He will complete us, filling the void and making us whole. Your life journey will be exciting, exhausting, terrifying, magical, terrible, and wonderful. We must remind ourselves that on the good days, we praise God, and on the awful days, we praise God, too.

In every day, there is a lesson to be learned, faith to be strengthened, and hope to hold onto. I hate when people say, "God won't give you anything you can't handle." That's a complete lie, and if anyone tells you that, tell them to stop. The truth is, God won't give you anything that you can't handle WITHOUT HIS HELP. The statement should go, "There is nothing that you and God *together* can't handle." There will be thousands of things you can't handle throughout your life. You will get discouraged, overwhelmed, anxious, and beat down by what life throws at you. Some days you will feel like you can't make it, BUT GOD. But God can do what we cannot do. But God can walk us through the fires. But God can part the waters and drown the enemies behind us. But God can give us a new name. But God can shut the mouths of the lions and take down the giant with a single stone. But God can wipe out an entire army with 300 men. But God can.

The reality of life, as we walk through this journey, is that no one gets out alive. During my intense panic attacks, I was so consumed with death and the fear of dying that I was afraid to live. It struck me one day that no matter how hard I fight it, how hard I try to control it, how hard I try to avoid it, death will come, and with it, new life with Christ. No one is getting out of here alive, so why not live?

If our Heavenly Father truly loves us, then He wouldn't make death mandatory, and He certainly wouldn't make death scary or something to fear. For goodness sake, He sent His own Son to die! I genuinely believe that the closer our relationship is with Jesus, the less scary death becomes.

Think of it this way—if you were told you had to move to another country and the only person going with you was your best friend, you probably wouldn't be so scared. In fact, you would probably think of it as an adventure. The same goes for our relationship with Jesus; if we allow ourselves to stay distant from Him, death will seem very scary and daunting when we reach the end; however, if we take the time to build up a relationship with Him and become best friends with Him, death becomes a transition where we move locations with our best friend, who will be there every step of the way.

In order to live out our testimony completely and fully, we need to let God be God and live according to His will on earth. That means we need to be okay with His plan, no matter what that looks like. We can spend the rest of our lives worried about the "what if's" and, at the end of our life, realize that we existed but never lived.

So, what do we do? We stop fighting for control because we never really even had it to begin with. We surrender to the fact that God is in control because He is God, and we are not. Then we make a decision here and now that no matter what happens, no matter how life turns out, we consciously decide that we are going to be ok, regardless of the events that lie ahead. (NIV, Romans 8:28), *"And we know that in all things God works for the good of those who love Him, who have been called according to His purpose."* In ALL THINGS, God works. He is in every second of your life, guiding, preparing, helping, holding, and loving YOU for exactly who you are. So let go and let God. Your testimony comes when you realize that it never was about you. It's about the wonderful Savior who loved you so much; He died for you so that you could spend eternal life with Him.

It's about how His love flows through you in order to touch the deepest, darkest parts of another's soul with the story of how you survived.

It's about how you fought the fight of your life because that's exactly what you had to do; you had to fight for your life every second of every day until your breakthrough came. Your breakthrough will now allow you to bless those still struggling around you; giving them hope that your God can do for them what He did for you.

So how do you live out your testimony of triumph? The Bible tells us in Isaiah 61:1-3 (NIV), *"The Spirit of the Sovereign Lord is on me, because the Lord has anointed me to proclaim good news to the poor. He has sent me to bind up the brokenhearted, to proclaim freedom for the captives and release from darkness for the prisoners,* (Verse 2) *to proclaim the year of the Lord's favor, and the day of vengeance of our God, to comfort all who mourn* (Verse 3) *and provide for those who grieve in Zion—to bestow on them a crown of beauty instead of ashes, the oil of joy instead of mourning, and a garment of praise instead of a spirit of despair. They will be called oaks of righteousness, a planting of the Lord for the display of His splendor."*

We are to bring hope to the hopeless, constantly giving good news to those in captivity, letting them know that they, too, can be freed from their anxiety, addiction, and depression. Most importantly, we have to be just like the oak planted to grow and show off the splendor and faithfulness of God. Everywhere we go, we should be a shining example of what the power of God can do in our life.

Ram Dass said it so beautifully, "We are all just walking each other home." Take your testimony and use it to free someone else, for there is no greater example of love than to take the time to walk through a struggle with another human being, letting Christ shine through the broken and cracked pieces of your life that He has put back together. In Japan, there is a technique to mend cracked and broken pottery with gold. The idea is that you learn to embrace your imperfections and appreciate the times that broke you, cracked you, and damaged you beyond what you thought was reparable.

Christ is the gold that fills the cracks in our brokenness He seals up the scars with a radiant glow so when others see us, they won't see a broken mess; they will see a uniquely made masterpiece shining with radiance and beauty. Your brokenness never defined you; your testimony, however, will be a part of God's legacy forever. Now, are you ready? Take a deep breath…let's begin.

# ENDING PRAYER

Heavenly Father, we come to You today grateful for every opportunity we have been given to love You more. We thank You for, in Your word, solidifying our identity and constantly reminding us of who we are.

We thank You for the anxious moments, the panic moments, and the depressed moments that have left us grasping onto the thinnest hem of Your robe as we struggle to make it through yet another day. Lord, during our weak days, we thank You for never leaving us.

We find strength in Your presence as we fight off every negative attack from the evil one, knowing that in Your name, every knee must bow in Heaven and on Earth. We thank You, Lord, for leaving us with the same power that raised Christ from the dead.

During the storms of life, we thank You for being in our boat and never allowing us to sink. In the middle of our moment, Lord, when the fires consume us, when the lions surround us, and when the waves confront us as the enemy chases us down with a vengeance, we thank You for meeting us in the middle of *that* moment. In the middle of our mess. In the middle of the moment where we feel less than worthy, the moment where we feel like giving up. The moment where we have nothing left but a whisper, You show up and deliver us. In the middle of the worst moment of our life, Lord, we thank You for being who You are, which is precisely everything we need.

We thank You, Lord, that You have never once forgotten us. That despite how we may feel, Your truth and promises will forever chase us down until they show themselves true in every aspect of our lives. On the days when we see only giants staring us down, we remind ourselves, Lord, that the giants are much smaller when we look at them through the lens of who You are.

In life, we thank You for giving us the Holy Spirit to guide our words and our minds as we navigate the muddy waters of life. We are forever thankful for the peace that surpasses all understanding, the most incredible gift Your Son gave.

As we continue our day, we remind ourselves that the Joy of the Lord is our strength. Where Your Joy is, the enemy has no power.

May the promises of Your word overtake us, Lord, and consume us at every angle giving hope to every second of our lives.

Finally, Lord, we are forever grateful for the gift of Your Son and the blood He shed to save us from all our shortcomings. You are an incredibly faithful God, and we are forever grateful for Your unconditional and unfailing love.

As You see us through each day, strengthen us more, guide us with clarity, and most of all, let our lives show the world how wonderful You are through our thoughts, words, and actions. May everyone we encounter leave our presence knowing a little more about You and a lot more about Your love.

We are forever grateful for Your healing and for giving us the opportunity to bring hope to those struggling around us.

–Amen

*"In fact, we felt sure we were going to die. But this made us stop trusting in ourselves and start trusting God, who raises the dead to life."* 2 –Corinthians 1:9 (CEV)

# ABOUT THE AUTHOR

Caitlin Daly, a native to the Eastern Shore of Maryland, found her calling as an author in 2021. Her book *Mentally Bankrupt* opens the reader to the harsh truths and raw emotions of dealing with panic attacks, anxiety, addiction, and depression. Realizing that walking through these struggles can be a very lonely walk, Caitlin wanted to break the barriers of isolation and bring hope, healing, and restoration to anyone struggling to find freedom. She is a firm believer that if God can help her, He can help anyone, for there is nothing too great for the Lord. When she is not public speaking, she enjoys spending free time with her daughter, exploring the outdoors, and creating mosaics. You can learn more about her and her journey by going to #DalyDoseOfHope on social media and YouTube.

# How to have a personal relationship with Jesus

Having a personal relationship with Jesus means that you freely accept Him as Lord and Savior over your life. Jesus has always been Lord and Savior, but you now acknowledge and accept this truth. You recognize and believe that He died so that your sins could be forgiven, and His death on the cross now allows you to rest with Him in Heaven one day.

If you have never prayed before, I urge you to use your own words, talk to God like a friend, and let Him into the deepest innermost parts of your soul. We don't need to use fancy words when talking to God; there are no rules when it comes to expressing our thoughts, feelings, and emotions to Him.

The Bible tells us to start our prayers by giving thanks, and from there, if and only if you genuinely feel sorry, repent your sins to God. (He already knows everything, so I don't suggest leaving details out during this confession.) Once you have confessed, ask God to come into your heart and tell Him that you are willing to leave your past behind so He can give you a new life and future with Him. I genuinely believe that when we are raw and honest with God, He can start to rebuild our lives.

If you don't have a church community, I urge you to look around your area and find one with a firm foundation on the Bible and God's truths (It's okay if you have to try out multiple churches until you find the right fit). Look for ways to incorporate God into your everyday life and enjoy the journey of getting to know God on a deeper level. Study your Bible and challenge yourself to follow Jesus' teachings. Every day is new, and this one, you are choosing to acknowledge Christ as your Savior! Today is a good day!

Welcome to the family of believers!

Founded in 2006, and now with over 3,150 wells drilled, Ken Wood's nonprofit charity to bring clean drinking water to the people of Ghana and Tanzania has become his passion. LWI's logo incorporates Ken's greatest belief that "Water is Life".

It's true… "You can't go back and change the beginning, but you can start where you are and change the ending." ~ C. S. Lewis

The mission of **Lifetime Wells International** and its cofounders, Ken Wood and David Powell, is to improve the quality of life for communities in Ghana and Tanzania by providing access to clean water and eliminate death and disease caused by drinking unsafe water.

The average cost to provide an entire community or school with a well is $3,500. We're grateful for the generosity of a small number of private donors who cover administrative costs, allowing 100% of other donations to fund water projects.

As of the spring of 2023, since its inception, Lifetime Wells Vision has provided help to those who needed vision improvements and gave sight back through 13,000 surgeries, approximately 13,000 pairs of glasses and 79,000 eye treatments, fulfilling God's call in the Bible:

*"I chose you to bring justice,*
*and I am here at your side.*
*I selected you and sent you*
*to bring light*
*and my promise of hope*
*to the nations.*
*You will give sight*
*to the blind;*
*you will set prisoners free*
*from dark dungeons."*
(Isaiah 42:6-7 - CEV)

10% of all book sales will go directly to Lifetime Wells International.

Made in the USA
Middletown, DE
21 January 2024